T0271951

Routledge Revivals

Towards Industrial Freedom

Originally published in 1917 in the midst of World War I, Carpenter argues that industry in pre-war Britain was simply exploitation of labour for private gain and attempts to look toward a future with more socialist values. The papers in this study explore the negative aspects of industrial life and suggest a new outlook with which the United Kingdom can move forward in industry. This title will be of interest to students of sociology.

Towards Industrial Freedom

Edward Carpenter

Routledge
Taylor & Francis Group

First published in 1917
by George Allen & Unwin Ltd

This edition first published in 2016 by Routledge
2 Park Square, Milton Park, Abingdon, Oxon, OX14 4RN
and by Routledge
711 Third Avenue, New York, NY 10017

Routledge is an imprint of the Taylor & Francis Group, an informa business

Publisher's Note
The publisher has gone to great lengths to ensure the quality of this
reprint but points out that some imperfections in the original copies may
be apparent.

Disclaimer
The publisher has made every effort to trace copyright holders and
welcomes correspondence from those they have been unable to contact.

A Library of Congress record exists under LC control number: 17031568

ISBN 13: 978-1-138-18392-6 (hbk)
ISBN 13: 978-1-315-64551-3 (ebk)

Towards
Industrial Freedom

BY

EDWARD CARPENTER

LONDON : GEORGE ALLEN & UNWIN, LTD.
RUSKIN HOUSE   40 MUSEUM STREET, W.C. 1
NEW YORK : CHARLES SCRIBNER'S SONS

First published in 1917

CONTENTS

TOWARDS INDUSTRIAL FREEDOM

I

INTRODUCTORY

ALTHOUGH the following papers were mostly
written before the Great War broke out, yet it
will be noticed that the consciousness runs through
them of a great impending crisis and transformation of our social arrangements, both in this
country and in Western Europe. It may not
have been clear at that time exactly *how* that
crisis would come about ; but now that the War
is on us we can see how inevitable in a sense it
has been, and how this deadly strife of nations
has flowed (in the main) from the hopeless falsity
of the social and industrial conditions prevailing
in the countries concerned—the falsity of undemo-
cratic societies divided into classes whose chief
object in life was to prey upon each other ; the
falsity of a so-called social order which ignored
the rights of women ; and the falsity of an industrial system whose *real* object was not public
welfare but private gain, not the production of
goods for use but the exploitation of labor for

profit.   Robbery and strife, more or less covered
over and concealed by canting phrases, have eaten
deep into the heart of these nations, and that over
a long period ; and now at last we see that it was
inevitable that some time this spirit of enmity
and inhumanity, this internal disease, which has
for so long afflicted us, should break forth and
come to the surface, if even in the thunder of
guns and the drenching of Europe with blood.

   In a way the fact that some of these causes of
disaster were traced and exposed (as they were
by many Socialist thinkers) long before the
disaster itself arrived, gives their exposure
additional validity and force.   Whatever side-
issues there may be in the present catastrophe,
we cannot doubt that financial greed and profit-
mongering, made all the more possible by the
domination of the profit-mongering classes, have
been at the bottom of the trouble.   The war began
with the speculative plotting of Germany for the
development of Mesopotamia and the Baghdad
Railway, and now England is apparently showing
her high moral disapproval of this by taking
over the development herself !   Whatever may
be thought about individual and isolated instances,
it is evident that commercial ambitions, and the
consequent demand for the annexation of territory, have for long enough in all the nations concerned been leading up to a crisis of deadly
conflict ; and the connexion of this with class-
domination is well illustrated by the fact that

Russia with the change of her Constitution has immediately repudiated the desire for annexation, while the Socialists of Germany and the other countries repudiate it also.[1]

But the long foreground of this tragedy, and its deep and intimate genesis out of the very heart and habits of the various nations, must persuade us of something else—namely that it is not destined to pass over very quickly ; and that its results will be profounder, longer-enduring and more far-reaching than we have even yet dared to imagine. Guglielmo Ferrero, the Historian of Republican Rome, points out in a late article in *Il Secolo*, the extraordinary shortsightedness of the views held about the present European situation by the politicians generally. " Great things," he says, " are maturing in the world. From one end to the other there is preparing the most gigantic trial or test (ordalia) that ever has been seen, of States, dynasties, nations, parties, religions and philosophical doctrines. It is like a universal Judgment day. Worldly crowns

---

[1] It is interesting to find that so long ago as 1805 a certain Dr. Hall writing on the evils of modern civilisation said : " In consequence of the rich of most of the different civilised nations of Europe all coveting the same things, the countries producing those things are the continual objects of contests and wars between these different powers. These wars are easily excited by the rich, who are either themselves the persons with whom lies the power of making war and peace, or are the persons who have great influence with those who have that power" (*The Effects of Civilisation on the People in European States*, by Charles Hall, M.D., 1805).

and powers, with their ancient glories, their idols, their altars and their faiths are apparently ready to roll in the dust " ; and yet while the one living idea which can save society is that of a new social order resting on reason and on justice " there have so far only appeared on the scene, old men, professing old ideas, making use of old principles, repeating ancient discourses, and seeming to be willing to do anything rather than change their old habits of the courtier, the official, and the Parliamentarian."

I have no intention here of entering into political questions ; but certainly in the social and industrial field the limitation of outlook among our British leaders is little short of astonishing. In all the talk lately about the renovation of the country after the war, about the finding of employment for returning soldiers, the planting of the people on the land or in industrial life, and so forth, it seems to be taken for granted that when things settle down again, our general industrial system will return as before : that " employers " will once more " find work " for their men, that the " employed " will be only too thankful to escape from prowling the streets ; and that (of course) nothing will be produced unless it yields a " profit " to some one—a dividend to a shareholder or a rent to a landlord. There seems to be no suspicion of the possibility of any other arrangement—or if there are suspicions they are indeed kept dark !

Similarly with regard to our foreign trade, great caucuses and conferences are being held with the object of diverting trade from its natural channels in such a way as to benefit ourselves and do despite to our " enemies." It is of course a case of trying to make water run uphill. Yet there seems to be no foresight of the fact that with the growing internationalisation of world-traffic (not to mention the growing internationalisation of the peoples themselves) such schemes are doomed to failure, or at most to a very short-lived success.

Nothing seems to me more certain than that our *whole* commercial system, both as regards internal economy and as regards foreign trade, is on its last legs, and that it is doomed to dissolution —or at least to such a transformation in spirit as will be equivalent to a dissolution of its present form. And surely such a dissolution is not only to be expected, but truly to be prayed for. After a career of a century and a half during which it has defiled the world with every kind of moral stain and physical ugliness, it is surely time that the Shop-keeping Age should pass away. Doubtless it has had, for its time, a function to fulfil —it has had uses in the winning for mankind of all sorts of external facilities and values, and in the scattering of " comforts and conveniences " —telephone- and water-closets and the like—all over the habitable globe ; but now surely it will be seen that its main use can only have been as a preparation for something infinitely *more* valuable, to come after.

As a matter of fact Bankruptcy, in more senses than one, impends over the nations of Europe, and it is curious, as Ferrero says, that, despite that obvious fact, the statesmen and politicians of the various countries go on playing the old trivial games, like gamblers in the midst of an earthquake, oblivious or unheeding that at any moment the house they are in may come tumbling about their heads.

In this country the absence of any real grasp of the situation among our leaders—even among our Labour-leaders—is *most* curious.   Mr. Bonar Law tells us, in a quite jaunty way, that we are spending £7,000,000 a day—but confesses that he has no effective knowledge of, or control over, the accounts.   Everything goes smoothly so far ; and there is a general impression that we " shall come out all right."   Certainly, just above Niagara the water does flow very smoothly, though with a swift and ever swifter course.   " Sit still and shut your eyes," says the War Office, " and we will censor the Press so that the public shall not be able to look ahead, even if it wants to."

And supposing for a moment that Bankruptcy (in the strictly financial sense) does *not* ensue. What then?   Why, for the United Kingdom so enormous a permanent debt that some 300 or 400 millions sterling will have to be paid yearly to the bondholders for the rest of mortal time !

Does any one for a moment suppose that the people of this country—already weighed down to the ground by mortgages, dividends, and taxation of all kinds—are going to bear this added burden, that they possibly *can* support it? Great as the sufferings would be which Bankruptcy would entail, they would not be a tenth of those caused by this alternative. And yet we talk glibly about " winning the War " !

Germany—whether in Socialist or Imperialist hands—will probably repudiate her debts. We might, if we like, say that being accustomed to tearing up scraps of paper she will make no great demur about doing so—and of course the fact of her debts being all internal, among her own people, will make this course easier. England will be more unwilling to repudiate, but may of course in the end be forced to do so. France will follow suit, and possibly also Italy and Russia. The Americans will be left to boss the world.

The outlook is not cheerful. But these and many other things all point to the same conclusion —the necessity of considering very seriously, as far as this country is concerned, what are to be its industrial forms in the future. I feel myself that to lay down any hard and fast doctrine on this subject would be rash. It would certainly be foreign to my intention. On the other hand we can see some very distinct directions in which men's minds are moving, and certain clear conditions for the coming organisations, without which we should not be satisfied ; and I have thought it best, in the following papers, to make suggestions with regard to these without attempting to be too Utopian or *doctrinaire*. The course of evolution is always difficult to forecast, and to turn beforehand even the very next page of the history of one's own country is impossible. Nevertheless, like a good sportsman, one can prepare oneself for every emergency, one can guess from the lie of the ground what game is likely to appear and with what kind of situation one may have to deal.

In the first of the following chapters I have sketched rather roughly the evils which arose from the industrial arrangements of the early part of the last century, and the reforms into which these evils forced us. In the later chapters I endeavour to infer what further transformations we may expect in the future. These transformations will, I take it, be largely of a psychological character— that is, they will depend on a changed mental attitude towards life, on a changed estimate of values, even more than on a change of institutions. When people come to value beauty in our daily life more than they do now, when they long intensely for that kind of industrial freedom which causes men's handiwork to become an art and a joy, when they perceive that the glory and the sweetness of the blue sky and a clean air are assets which we cannot neglect without peril to our souls and bodies, when they understand that

co-operation is not only valuable because it increases the productive efficiency of men, but much
more valuable when it liberates their dormant
instinct of mutual helpfulness and love—when they
see that all these inner things and many others
are of more importance for human happiness than
the mere increase of external riches—then indeed
the Shop-keeping Age will have passed away.
It is with a view to this psychological transformation that I have gathered together in this volume
papers on " Industry as an Art," on " Beauty in
Everyday Life," on " Non-Governmental Society,"
" Agricultural Co-operation," and so forth.

It becomes increasingly evident, I think, that
over and beyond any formulas of reform what is
needed is a *new spirit* of social and industrial life.
Without that even the best institutions will be of
little avail.   As Mr. Clutton Brock says : " The
desire for spiritual freedom is the basis, the only
basis, for Socialism. . . . And Socialism should
endeavour to prove that it is the natural and
inevitable product of the desire for spiritual freedom."   This spiritual freedom means the opportunity to evolve from oneself what one thinks right
and true and beautiful.   It means a co-operation
of all the members of society, and this in a
way not merely technical and external, but in
a real spirit of mutual help and equality.   Only
on such conditions, we may be sure—only on the
condition of spiritual and creative freedom—can
a society be really human and healthy.

At the conclusion I have introduced a long paper on " Social and Political Life in China " —partly because I think the study of the conditions that exist in a land so remote in every way from our own may (especially at this time when our own institutions are in the melting-pot) be of great assistance.   When one reflects that China has come down unbroken through a period of over forty centuries, and with her general polity during that period very *little* altered ; that she has survived internal convulsions and the shocks of Time and the external attacks of many nations ; one cannot refuse to see that there must be something very substantial and very well worth studying in that spirit which has inspired her and those institutions which she has adopted.   It has been the fashion of a cheap Western criticism to ridicule China and to represent her as enduring agelong in a state of slumber and fatuity.   Apart from the improbability of such a theory, it is absolutely rejected by all those travelers who have made the land of Sinim a subject of intimate and prolonged study, nor do all the foolish political efforts of the Western nations during the last seventy or eighty years, and their complete failure to break up that great Organism, lend any countenance to the theory.   China is as strong to-day as she ever was—as the world will presently find out. And as an instance of the value and power of the general public spirit ruling a nation in comparison with formal laws and institutions I may here mention one thing. In China it is thought rather disgraceful to live on the rent of land. There is no law, as I understand, against it, but there is a strong public opinion—and though, as a matter of convenience, it is not uncommon for one small holder who has more than he wants to rent out an acre or two to another who has less, it is really rare for any one to attempt or to dare to live entirely from the tribute of his tenants. In England, I need hardly remark, it is just the opposite ; there is a common public opinion in the other direction, and a man is respected, and even thinks himself respectable, just in pro- portion to the length of his rent-roll. Apart then from all legislation one can see in these two instances the vastly differing results of a differing spirit of life—in China an immense and far-flung peasant-class rooted comfortably in small tenures on the land, the most productive and the most stable on the whole Earth, and in England huge private estates half cultivated by a paralysed and inefficient population, and a country in perpetual danger on account of the inadequacy of its food- supply.

As there has been a recrudescence lately of the effort to break up Trade Unions I have included in the Appendix a paper on " The Minimum Wage," showing the valuable and indeed indispensable work the Unions have done, if only in the establishment of this principle.

THE TRANSFORMATION OF OUR INDUS-
TRIAL SYSTEM

ABOUT the middle of last century there arose a
great belief that the world was somehow going to
be saved by Trade and Commerce. With the rise
of the huge Machine-industries in the end of the
eighteenth century, and the immense development
of Locomotion in the early part of the nineteenth,
the commerce of the world increased by leaps
and bounds. The Crystal Palace in 1851 was
the first of a series of Exhibitions which were
held as monuments and milestones   human
industrial progress. The lines of the Railways
and Steamships, spreading rapidly like a wonderful web over the world, linked land to land ; and
it was said, and said again, " Leave these forces
to their natural issue, let each man pursue his
own profit his own interest—each country the
same—and by the inevitable operation of trade
and industrial exchange the whole world will ere
long be united in one great Brotherhood. The
Sheffield forger and grinder will manufacture
sickles for Russia ; and the Russian peasant,

cutting his wheat crop with the same, will send back a portion of it for the sustenance of the Sheffielder. The Lancashire girl working in the mills, and helping to turn out cotton goods by the mile for the natives of India, will run home in the evening, with shawl thrown over her head, to her little cottage, and sit down to a cup of tea whose leaves have been plucked by her dark-skinned sister in the tea-gardens of Assam " Tennyson, who more than any other poet gave voice to this period and these aspirations, said in a passage often since quoted :—

For I dipt into the future, far as human eye could see,
Saw the Vision of the world, and all the wonder that would be,
Saw the heavens fill with Commerce, argosies of magic sails,
Pilots of the purple twilight, dropping down with golden bales,

   .   .   .   .

Till the war drum throbbed no longer, and the battle flag was furled,
In the Parliament of man, the Federation of the world.

It was a glorious dream, this apotheosis of Commerce ! this vision of an international Brotherhood founded on trade and barter ! And who shall say that, *in a sense*, it may not some day be fulfilled—that some day earth's children may not in freedom create and in freedom and friendliness interchange, the products of their labors? But so far, alas ! the dream has *not* been fulfilled. The Trade and the Commerce truly exist. But the freedom and the friendliness—where are they? Only wage-slavery, and the nations and the peoples armed to the teeth in enmity against each other.

And the reason why the dream has not been fulfilled is clear enough. You cannot make a silk purse out of a sow's ear. And out of a Trade and a Commerce founded on greed and self-seeking, and chicanery, and the law of devil-take-the-hindmost, you cannot get, and you cannot expect to get, a society of brotherhood and trust and mutual help. The spirit has been deficient from the beginning ; and the tree will bear no other fruit than its own seed.

From the beginning, and before Tennyson, there were warning voices. Thoreau, from his New England hermitage, said, " Trade curses everything it handles," and again, " I have tried Trade ; but found it would take ten years to get on in that, and that then I should probably be on my way to the devil." And before him again, Shelley in his youthful inspiration of *Queen Mob* spoke of

> Commerce ! beneath whose poison-breathing shade
> No solitary virtue dares to spring ;
> But Poverty and Wealth with equal hand
> Scatter their withering curses.

Strong words !—perhaps even a trifle over-charged—but alas ! how true, how true in the main, even down to to-day !

It may be worth while to consider some of the ways or respects in which this modern Commerce has proved itself a failure—as thus supplying us with some hints towards the future. And first I will take its foundation principle of *Internecine Competition*.

Now every one will allow that Competition, in the sense of a reasonable emulation in good work and efficiency, is a very sensible and proper thing. But it must be remembered that the Political Economists and the Industrial leaders of the early nineteenth century went far beyond this. They laid it down, in their great principle of *laissez-faire*, that no restraint should be placed upon individual effort in the midst of the great struggle for existence—and even that if every man (short of actually breaking the law) went straight for his own advantage, regardless of others, the total result for society at large would be favorable and harmonious. In consequence of this doctrine—or rather, perhaps, in concurrence with it—came a period of the wildest competition—in which, in the struggle for Trade and for Profit, almost every law, human and moral (which did not happen to be written in the Statute Book), was broken ; and in which the sufferings of those trampled underfoot in the struggle—the suffering of women and tiny children in the coal-mines, of strong men in glass-works and steel-works, of girls in chemical works and cotton mills, of chimney-sweeps, of farm-laborers, of sweated workers in city slums, and so forth—were so frightful, that in spite of the theories of the Professors, and the fierce protests of the great Lords of trade,[1] the nation insisted from time to time on new Statute-laws restraining and restricting the freedom of the strong man as against the weak, and defining and defending equitable relations between employer and employed. Thus the later part of the nineteenth century and the whole Victorian era witnessed a slow but inevitable reaction against *laissez-faire* ; and so ensued the very decided, though mostly unacknowledged, beginnings of our modern socialism.

This period of wild competition, and the readjustment under it of all industrial relations, is perhaps unique in human history. In all the old societies—look where you will—you will find individualistic competition having a very restricted sway. The old societies were mainly *customary*. Trade in old days was a matter of custom. The word "customer" indicates this. If you dealt with one man for your boots, and with another for your bread, and with another for your meat, you were the customer of these various people ; the prices too were customary ; and these forms of custom were not changed except for strong and necessary reasons. In any one district there established itself in consequence a kind of equili-

[1] Even John Bright in 1847 protested against the limiting of women's and children's labor to ten hours *per diem.*

brium; and each tradesman could know pretty clearly what his prospect and outlook for the coming year might be. But with the coming-in of the world-wide Trade of which we are speaking all this was changed. The Sheffield cutler who, with his forbears, had manufactured table knives for centuries suddenly found a deluge of such knives coming in from Germany; the Coventry watchmaker discovered that watches were pouring in from Switzerland or Massachusetts; the farmer stared in dismay at sacks of flour arriving from Canada or the Danubian plains, and at thousands of heads of cattle consigned from the Argentine. Prices were hopelessly cut down and mangled, and men who had before been making a fairly prosperous and reliable living found themselves plunged in failure and debt. At the same time the world-wide Trade brought new sources of employment; great new industries sprang up; the wage-working populations migrated from place to place in search of new work. The old steady-going humdrum order of things was shattered, and in its place there set in a confused but fierce struggle —men dislocated from their old occupations fighting with each other at the doors of factories and workshops for admittance; masters underselling each other in the home and foreign markets; employers, in order to keep their footing against rivals, beating down the wages of their own men to the lowest possible point; and the workers, in order to keep body and soul together, banding with each other to fight the employers.

It is in the midst of this cut-throat commercial warfare that we have been living. No one can look out upon the Industrial World of to-day without seeing that it is so. And no one can look upon it without seeing that to continue living in it is intolerable—that things cannot remain as they are. It is a time of Transition. The old customary order of society is behind us ; the rational and humane order lies in front ; and it is towards this latter that we have to press on.

The second instance of the failure of Modern Commerce which I will take is that of *Fraud and Adulteration*, with their inevitable accompaniment, *Waste*.

In the old social order, in which production was local, and the origin of nearly all articles consumed was well-known to those who consumed them, there was not much room for this trouble. The coat one wore was certified in all respects. Its wool came from a neighboring farmer's sheep, and was spun into yarn by some village grandmother ; it was woven into cloth on a cottage loom, and made up into a garment by the parish tailor or the local housewife. If there were scamping or deceit anywhere it was pretty sure to be found out. If the local pork butcher displayed an unwonted abundance of sausages, and at the same time there occurred a mysterious disappearance of the neighbors' cats, it was easy to put two and two together, and to affix the blame and the discredit ! But when the world-wide Trade came in, all this was changed. Fraud and Adulteration became positively practicable, comparatively safe, and superlatively profitable, and the rush in that direction became so enormous that to catalogue all the forms these evils took would be simply impossible. Books like *The Jungle* and *Tono-bungay* have familiarised the world with certain aspects. Years ago Herbert Spencer pointed out that silk goods were commonly loaded with such heavy dyes as to convert 1 lb. of pure silk into $2\frac{1}{2}$ lb. of the marketable commodity ! To-day (I have reason to know) there are " pure linen " goods turned out in Manchester which are made entirely of cotton, with an admixture of size ! And so far has this habit penetrated that (according to Phil May) the little slum-girl nowadays, who buys half a pound of margarine from the grocer says : " And please, Sir, mother says, would you stamp the *cow* on it, as we have company coming to tea? "

The progress of science has reached such a point, and the chemicalising of products has become so subtle, that inspection and regulation are non-plussed, and the pursuing of the evil by Law is plainly seen to be only, a temporary remedy—which must ultimately give way before the only radical cure, namely the merging of this unholy scramble of the markets in a serene and orderly form of communal production.

And under this head it is perhaps not unfair to dwell for a moment on the whole present system of Advertisements and Travelers. A few years ago (1901) it was calculated that in Great Britain alone 80,000 folk were employed in the advertisement trade, besides 64,000 commercial travelers. How near these various activities run to the line of Fraud we must leave the parties concerned to judge, but of their signification as illustrating the intolerable Waste of our present system every one can form an opinion. For all this vast expense of labor and treasure represents only the internecine warfare of firms with one another —each bent on destroying its rival or rivals— and whatever Trade one firm gains in the process is lost by some other, so that the total advantage or profit to the community is absolutely zero. Many years ago Mr. Pears boasted that he spent £100,000 a year in advertisements ; and now probably the sum is far larger. But of all the hundreds of thousands of pounds thus spent in the British soap trade what advantage does the community reap—except that its soap is so much dearer in consequence? The public in fact, through this extra price, pays and supports the great army of travelers and advertisers. But

far wiser and better off would the public be
if, instead, it simply planked down the same sum
in some such other way, as would provide the
said army with really useful work—useful to
themselves and to the community. And if any
one is so futile as to maintain that by this enormous expense of advertisement and travelers the
public is enabled to judge the merits of various
soaps for various uses, the obvious answer is that
a jury of washerwomen for a few pounds a year
could fulfil this function for all practical purposes
with the greatest ease and efficiency—and probably with far more satisfaction to the general
customer.

The third trouble which I wish to consider in
connection with Modern Industry is the *Fluctuation of Trade*. This is a very serious matter,
and one which I think will demand more attention in the future than it has hitherto received.
We saw that in the old society, when custom
ruled and production was local, industrial conditions were comparatively steady. Changes of
course took place ; but they were slow and
partial and there was fair time for readjustment.
Now on the contrary changes are rapid, sweeping, and unexpected. A small margin of profit
flings a whole body of trade across the Atlantic ;
a new invention, as we have already seen,
paralyses a whole industry in one place, and sets
it humming and buzzing in another. The country

boot-maker in old days supplied his own locality year in and year out with a certain class of hand-made article.   Now suddenly arrives from Northampton or perhaps from New England a consignment of machine-made boots at break-neck prices ; and he sees ruin staring him in the face.   A sense of painful Insecurity affects all the trades, small or large, in the country or in the town.   It becomes impossible to fore-cast the future.   At any moment these causes of fluctuation may arise.   The employer suffers ; he is timid and anxious ; he fears to lay down capital.   The worker suffers ; he is haunted by the prospect of the " sack," and the long weary walking of the streets.

This fluctuation is a great evil.   We may say that however bad conditions may be, yet if they are *fixed* human ingenuity and necessity will presently devise a way to make the situation tolerable.   If for instance the demand for British coal suddenly fell to only one half of the present demand, and remained there, and *it was known that it would remain at that low figure*, then— although for the moment there would be disloca-tion and great suffering—yet in a short time the excess of coal workers would migrate elsewhere and those that remained would soon continue working under normal conditions.   But when the fluctuations are continual and unforeseen, the pain so caused in the body politic is extreme.   At one moment men are drawn in thousands to a district, only a few months later to be starved out for want of employment, and cruelly dispersed to other centres. A kind of alternate inflammation and atrophy of industrial tissue takes place, and the consequent pain and anxiety to all concerned, both employers and employed, are terrible. One result, as far as the employers are involved, is the abandonment of " stocking." With the swift fluctuations of demand for any class of goods, due to world-wide Trade (and collaterally also to new Fashions and new Inventions), the manufacturer does not to-day venture to lay in a large stock or store of any one article, lest with the cessation of demand it be thrown useless on his hands. He knows there is always a great army of unemployed waiting outside his gates (and modern Industry and Manufacture positively now depend and rely on this fact) ; and he sees that for his purpose the best plan is to live from hand to mouth, as it were—to just supply the demand of the moment, if necessary by calling in extra workers from outside ; and then when that is over, and the ebbtide comes, to discharge a lot of hands, taking them (or others) on again later when a boom occurs. In the old days of course fluctuations were much less in extent and slower in operation ; and those that did occur were greatly alleviated by the custom of stocking, by which in slack times the work was continued much as usual, and the surplus of stock thus created was stored up to be ready for the

next busy season. In those days old hands were
seldom discharged, and new ones were but slowly
taken on ; and the Industrial machine ran
smoothly and evenly, like an engine with a big
fly wheel. But now with the abandonment of
stocking the jolting and self-destruction of the
whole organism are terrible and ruinous.

With the constant " on and off " of employment which our general industrial system entails,
the condition of large masses of the workers is
fatally bad. If their wages when actually in
work are fair, yet their total and average in the
long run are wretchedly small ; saving becomes
hopeless ; long periods of unemployment occur ;
and the effect on the *character* of the man is
most baneful. The sufferings entailed in the
process are so great, that he loses his courage,
he loses hope and object in life, he loses the
habit of steadfast industry, and in cases where
ill-fortune continues he loses actual skill and
efficiency. Finally, if a long period of want of
employment brings about the break-up of the
home and the adoption of the life of the tramp,
the tragedy of this transition is so great that (as
statistics show) a return afterwards to normal
life is rarely possible. The man becomes adapted
to an aimless existence. " *When* shall I get
work again? " inquired the needy workman of the
old fortune-teller. " You will have bad luck
for two or three years," said she, " but after
that . . ." " Yes, after that? " hurriedly asked

the anxious querist. "*You will get used to it!*" was the fatal reply.

Such are some of the awful problems which loom up in connexion with modern industrial life, and make us feel that we are nearing the end of one dispensation, and must be preparing for the arrival of another. The present system hastens to its crisis and its close. As competition becomes keener and keener, as the world-wide Trade draws its currents from farther and farther shores, so does the whirlpool at the centre become more and more fatally swift. Every day the machines spin faster and faster, every day the " drive " in the workshops is intensified. Production of wealth increases with enormous strides, and every day with less actual cost of labor. Thus it comes about that while the needs of the world are being supplied by the toilers, and an enormous portion of the wealth so produced is being appropriated by the shareholder and the landlord, the actual number of wage-receivers in the process is if anything being reduced. As the machines spin faster, in fact, so much faster do they throw off on the one hand the unemployed poor, and on the other hand the unemployed rich.

This double problem of unemployment is the master problem of our time, and its solution the key to the future. It is both a threat and a hope. For the failure to solve it will mean the ruin and destruction of modern society ; it will

mean the continued and increased production of
futile and imbecile crowds on the surface and in
the upper ranges of social life, and the continued
and increased production of hopeless and despair-
ing crowds of incompetents in the lower ranges
—a double burden which, unremoved, must
inevitably crush Society beneath it. But the
solution of the problem will lead the way to the
promised land of a new era.[1]

The sufferings of the unemployed—to any one
who at all knows them—have indeed been very
terrible—terrible even to think of. But there is
this hope in them, that these very woes have
forced the attention of the world, they have compelled us at last to face the problems which lie
behind them, and are the origin of them. The
man who stands at the dock-gates asking not
for alms but for a pittance of *work*, and stands
there, ill-clothed and ill-fed, for hours and hours
in the rain and cold, if so he may win bread
for his little ones, is (though we do not always
see it so) the Christ knocking at the door of
modern society, knocking at the door of our
hearts. He is ourself in another guise. Long
have we turned a deaf ear, long have we hardened
our hearts. But now we can do so no longer.
For humanity's sake, for the sake of our common
life, we must open the gates and let him in.

And this opening of the gates—what is it? It
is the acknowledgment of his *Right to Work*.

[1] See Appendix.

Let us pause on this a moment. Some folk would deny that there can be any such right, as a right to work. But surely if they deny that, in a society constituted as ours is, they deny the existence of *any* right. For a man can ask no more modest, no more reasonable, no more unassailable right than the *right to support himself*. Observe, it is not the right to beg that is claimed, though that to a starving man can hardly be denied ; it is not the right to steal, or in some way to live on the labor of others, though that is certainly claimed and taken by large sections of society ; it is not the right even to be supported out of the rates, though that is granted by the Poor Law. No, it is a claim much more modest and humble than any of these—simply the right to have an opportunity of earning one's own living !

And can such a claim be resisted?—The more we think about it, and the more Society at large thinks about it, the more we see that in all reason and humanity it cannot be resisted.

But some say : We admit that the claim in itself seems a reasonable one, but the real difficulty is this, that there is no practicable way in which the claim can be granted—in which work can actually be provided, however willing we may be to provide it. To such objectors we may reply :—Very well, then, if we can show that there are many ways in which self-supporting work can be provided, you will surely feel bound to adopt

3

them, or at least to make sincere and thorough trial of them.

That methods can be found by which, after the lapse of a few preparatory years, remunerative work could be provided for everybody—and with great general advantage to the whole community —there can be no reasonable doubt. Any one who has looked into the subject must I think agree to this. The real doubt lies in the willingness of those at present in power to adopt the methods—and the reason for this unwillingness I will refer to later. For the moment let us consider what these methods are.

In the face of the detailed and masterly handling of this subject in the Minority Report of the Poor Law Commission it would be superfluous for me to enter into them very minutely, as well as impossible within the limits of this paper. Suffice it to say that the main points are (1) The gradual shortening of the working day—especially to begin with, in public industries like the Railway, tram and omnibus services ;[1]   (2) the diminution of Boy and Girl labor, and the raising of the School age ;[2] (3) the institution of great and ultimately greatly remunerative public works, like Afforestation and

[1] See *The Remedy for Unemployment*, being Part II. of the Minority Report of the Poor Law Commission (Fabian Society, 1909), p. 275.
[2] Ditto, p. 269.

Land Reclamation ; [1] (4) the founding of Labor and Farm Colonies.[2]

Most of these points explain themselves. The shortening of the hours of labor would cause an absorption of extra workers into those industries in which such shortening was carried out. The curtailing of Boy and Girl labor and the raising of the School age would, of course, not only cause an extra demand for adult labor, but would give an opportunity for the methodical technical training of young folk, and the turning them out into the world as efficient citizens—a most important matter. With the institution of great and permanent Government works of Reclamation, Afforestation, Canal restoration, extension, etc., not only would there be a great *increase* of employment, but it could be arranged—as the Minority Report recommends—that such works should proceed more rapidly in seasons of general Trade depression, and less rapidly in seasons of prosperity, so as in this way to counteract in some degree the *fluctuations* of general industry, which we have seen to be so harmful. And by the foundation of Labor and Farm colonies industrial training could be provided—compulsory in some cases, but voluntary in most—for those who are now incompetent and unskilled ; while by degrees and with extended experience and improvement in the general level of skill and

[1] Ditto, p. 280.
[2] Ditto, pp. 301, 328, and 329.

efficiency, such places could be rendered quite self-supporting and even remunerative.

A word upon this last point. The Minority Report, wisely perhaps, does not dwell upon the question of self-supporting colonies. The English labor colonies, like Hollesley Bay—largely owing to their half-hearted management—have not been a great success ; but the work done on the Continent in this line has been quite remarkable ; and already it. has become clear that in certain places of this kind—like Merxplas in Belgium— very inefficient human material, which in England becomes a heavy charge upon the rates, may be taken and rendered " practically self-support- ing " ; [1] while in other cases, as at Witzwill in Switzerland, similar material, well fed and lodged and gradually trained, yields an actual balance to the good, after all the expenses of the estab- lishment have been paid.[2]

Both these colonies, just mentioned, are of a more or less compulsory character, and deal with material of most unlikely kind—inefficient, un- willing, and constantly fluctuating. And the question arises whether, with these results obtained in such places, we may not fairly look forward to the founding of other Colonies of really skilled

[1] See *The Unemployed* : *a National Question*, by Percy Alden, price 1s. (P. S. King, 1905), p. 23.

[2] For an account of Witzwill Colony, see article by Edith Sellers, in the *Nineteenth Century* for January 1910.

and alert workers in all departments—Industrial
Villages and Garden Cities we might call them
—which should be greatly successful and prosperous, and yield a high rate of wages or return
for their labor to those co-operating in them.[1]
That skilled and efficient men and women must
be able—with all modern appliances and industrial science—to produce from the ground, and
supply each other with all the necessaries of life
and an abundance over and above, is, one may
say, a truism of Social economy. And for the
success of some such experiment all that would
seem really necessary would be the provision of
an ample area of land, and of a wise and experienced management. (After all, England itself,
taken as a whole, *is* such a colony—only very
badly organised, or scarcely at all, and with a
vast number of quite helpless and useless members
—and yet it supports itself year by year with a
perfectly astonishing superfluity and profit.)

In all this matter we have to remember that
reaping—as we are now doing—the harvest of
our unholy commercial system of the last century
or more, we cannot expect all at once to undo
its ill-effects and dissipate its deadly accumula-
tion of dregs below and of scum above. There

[1] A very interesting account of the large and highly
successful *voluntary* colony at Frederiksoord in Holland, is
given by Herbert V. Mills in his book, *Poverty and the State*
(price 1s.), pp. 148–54.

must necessarily be a considerable period of preparation, and of training of these helpless crowds to become useful and efficient. But once that is allowed, and it is understood that in the near future practically every boy and girl that comes of age will be qualified to do useful work for the community—why the nightmare about the difficulty or impossibility of *finding employment* will surely vanish quite naturally.

Why then—it may be asked—why are not efforts made at once to work out such proposals as above outlined, for the provision and extension of employment? Why are not large schemes adopted in the direction of shortening the working day, the curtailing of juvenile labor, the institution of great national and remunerative public works? Why is not serious consideration given to the subject of industrial villages—to be composed of efficient workers of all trades (of whom there may soon again be thousands walking about the streets)—while in the meantime other preparatory colonies, not entirely self-supporting, and the technical schools, might be tackling the problem of qualifying the young and the inefficient for the future time when they will be able to take their place as worthy and useful citizens? Every one admits the urgency of the Unemployment problem, they " deeply sympathise "—and yet, and yet, when these simple and obvious remedies are put forward, they are somehow ignored ! Why is it?

The answer is simple—and instructive. It is

because all these remedies involve the idea of industry being carried on not for Profit but for Use—not for the profit and gain of an individual man, a shareholder, a bondholder, a landlord—but for the use and advantage of the workers and the whole community ; and this idea is so appalling that it dislocates people's minds—and they cease to think : just as people cease to walk when their legs are dislocated ! Folk are so accustomed in fact to think that industry can only go on when it pays a big man to get a big profit out of it—they are so ingrained to our commercial system—that some of them genuinely believe that no other state of affairs is possible ; while others (not so innocent) see in any such change the *beginning of the end of legalised robbery* ! To such folk the reclamation of vast lands from the sea and the dotting them over with farm-steads and a prosperous population seems a useless and meaningless enterprise, for it would give no scope for speculation, nor yield any profit to individual shareholders ; the same of a home-colony ; while the shortening of the working-day in the various trades would certainly bring a danger of some slight diminution of dividends, and therefore, however important it might be for the health or safety of the workers, ought decidedly to be opposed.

Such then is the state of affairs in the United Kingdom to-day. The Commercial system and

the commercial ideals of the last century have
had their full fling ; and while creating a Trade
and a Wealth perfectly astounding and unparal-
leled (as, for instance, Total exports and imports
in 1830, £88,000,000 ; the same in 1907,
£957,000,000), they have at the same time
developed evils and inhumanities so monstrous
(e.g. Fraud and Adulteration unprecedented,
Robbery of the poor by the rich, vast accumula-
tions of diseased wealth, deadly masses of
Poverty) that it is felt that the process *cannot*
and *must* not any longer continue. And yet at
the same time, so ingrained is the habit of the
past—so persuaded are the workers that the only
source of employment is the self-interest and
speculative advantage of "masters," so determined are the employing classes not to
countenance any industry which does not yield
them dividends—that the next steps, which are
of course in the direction of production for Use,
though perfectly obvious, seem strange and almost
impossible.

It is evident that nothing but a new conception and spirit will avail—nothing but a new
germinating principle of industrial life. For, as
said before, the tree will bear no other fruit than
its own seed. We cannot get grapes from
thorns. Out of the seed of the plant called
devil-take-the-hindmost, sown in the beginning of
last century, has sprung for this age no ordered
and gracious social life, of friendliness and

humanity, of beauty and of joy, but only a wilder-
ness of briars—as any one may plainly see who
merely glances around. Briars, vigorous perhaps,
strong-growing, and covering all the land—but
after all, only briars. Nothing but the grafting
of a new life upon these, a new spirit, a new
germinating principle, will so transform them that
they will blossom at last into the rose of our
devotion and our love.

And this change, this new inspiration (which
is already coming to us) is coming, as ever,
from the outcast and the rejected. It is from
the pitiful figures scarce able to hold their rags
together, who flit past us like ghosts in the midnight of the richest city of the world, or huddle
crouching on the riverside seats—or from those
dreary cues of hopeless thousands who wait at
dockyard and factory gates—that the congregated
cry of suffering has gone up, which is at last
awakening the slumbering soul of our modern
civilisation to its human destiny, its real life.
" Abandon this mad, this inhuman struggle," it
says, " in which we and such as we are hourly
and eternally crucified—in which your own hearts
and lives are blasted. Look on us, and know
that we are but yourselves in another form.
Grant our claim, so unassailable, so elementary—
the simple Right to Work—that we may be
allowed to support ourselves—that the industrial
machine may be so modified that *all* may bear
their part, and none be excluded. Do this, and

lo ! in the hour that you do it you will have sown the Seed of a new Society—as far superior to the present one as the perfect rose is superior to the bramble—the society in which industry shall actually be carried on for human Use instead of for fraud and robbery.

" But do it not, and the hour of your ruin is at hand. The writing is already on the wall. No nation can continue for long, without serious disaster, to harbor huge masses of its population in a decaying and diseased state—forbidden from the land and all the conditions of healthy industry and life—its very own limbs and members mortify ing. The crisis draws rapidly near. Whether it comes from within, by the disorganisation of your own internal affairs, or whether from without, by direct foreign attack—unless you set your house in order, and that right soon, a great catastrophe awaits you."

This element, then, in the breakdown of our present Commercial system—this strange and ominous evolution of huge masses of unemployed poor and unemployed rich—is bringing us such a lesson as the above, and pointing us such a cure, largely on what may be called the moral plane. Another element in the same—namely the evolution of great industrial Trusts and Combines—is pointing a strictly practical direction for us to take, and a practical means by which we may possibly pass to the new Society.

The Trust of course is the halfway house to

the Public Administration of Industry. It prepares the way—in those larger wholesale industries to which it applies—for their being taken
over and administered by the Public.   Yet to
say '' prepares the way '' is hardly correct, seeing
that for years now, as already pointed out, legislation has gone in the direction of Socialism,
that is to say of restraining the wild race of
commercialism and introducing human order
where before was a self-seeking chaos for
years, too, it has gone in the direction of
municipalising industries and taking them over
into public control ; and of necessity it has done
so, for there is no other direction to-day in which
progress in such matters can well take place.
The Labor and Socialist parties in the State
have recognised and acknowledged this necessary
movement, and are deliberately and consciously
helping it on ; the Liberal and Conservative
parties, with their eyes more or less shut, do
not perhaps always know what they are doing,
or see where they are going ! yet the Statute
Book of the last 60 years shows plainly enough
—from the Ten Hours Act for women and children
of 1848 to the Minimum Wage and Wage-boards
Act of 1908 [1]—and it is too late *now* for these
parties to make a bogey of a movement which
they themselves have been nursing so long.

The advance, the growth, the conquest of the
general socialist conception are assured.   The

[1] See Appendix for Note on the Minimum Wage.

gradual transformation of our industries and
activities is inevitable—so that they will be carried
on in the main for public advantage and use.
How far the process begun in the Post Office,
the Telegraphs, Telephones, Railways, Trams,
Electricity, Gas, and Water Supply (not to
mention Munitions and the general Regimentation connected with the Great War)—how far
exactly Nationalisation and Municipalisation will
go—we cannot of course yet see. Certain
it is that before long the greater portion of the
land and the greater number of the large
industries will be collectively handled. And
certain it is that these changes will bring a
considerable alleviation of the evils of the
commercial era.

Public administration allays the evil of exces-
sive Competition, and the cut-throat warfare and
waste which go on still in the outside trades.
(Imagine for a moment what the Post Office
would be to-day if in the hands of a hundred
little competing letter-carrying firms !) Public
Administration practically puts an end to the evil
of Adulteration ; it curbs an enormous amount
of Fraud and Waste. Under it, Fluctuations
of employment, which we have seen to be so
great a curse, are much more easily controlled ;
Hours can be shortened at need, and sections
of unemployed so absorbed ; Wages and conditions made much more equable and favorable or just to the worker ; and in general the

Robbery of the poor by the rich minimised and gradually extinguished.

But—and this is a most important " but "— it brings with it the very great danger of the growth of officialism, bureaucracy, and red-tape, than which, if allowed free sway, few things can be more fatal to the real life of a nation. The multiplication of officials—as has been seen in the past history of Russia—strangles the spontaneous vitality of the people ; it creates a vast body of parasites, as bad as the dividend-drawing parasites of Commercialism ; and betrays the public into the power of a class hostile to change and to progress.

We see this alas ! only too clearly in connexion with the present War. In this country officialism is tightening its grip in a fateful way ; and administered as it is from above by a class which is out of touch and sympathy with the needs of the people it is becoming a great danger. The ignorance displayed by the War Office and the high Civil authorities concerning the common and necessary conditions of life among the masses is something astonishing ; it has led to perpetual altering of regulations and to every kind of vacillation and uncertainty ; it has bred a deep distrust in the minds of the people, and in this hour of national crisis, if carried much farther, might easily lead to something like revolution. At a time when national unity is above all things needed, the tendency to treat the unions and other

bodies of workers in a   superior ' and hostile
spirit—bodies that in general know fully as much
about the subjects in discussion and are quite
as ' patriotic ' as those who criticise them—and
the unwillingness to take these bodies into con-
fidence and work *with* instead of against them,
are signs of a most foolish and mistaken state
of mind.

As an instance of the kind of thing that is
constantly happening, I may perhaps quote from
a late book of mine a passage concerning the
shipping strike on the Clyde in 1910 : " A good
deal of indignation had been expressed up and
down the country at the conduct of the men in
the shipyards, who had refused to take up their
tools and go to work again, even after their
leaders had counselled and even urged them to
do so. I was as much in the dark as most
others about the cause of this strange refusal—
until I reached Greenock ; and then I soon heard
from various quarters, both of men and masters,
the real reason. It was not a question of wages
or of hours. Those matters had so far been
settled satisfactorily. The real grievance was a
personal one. The men had been affronted by
the overbearing conduct of the Chairman of the
Employers' Association, the insulting manner in
which he had behaved to their representatives,
and so forth ; and they were not going to put
up with this without a protest. They wanted
to be treated in a gentlemanly way. It was

encouraging and refreshing to find that this was so ; and the fact that it was so lets a good deal of light into a frequent cause of labor troubles and dissensions. But of course in this case at Greenock, as in so many others, the Press all over the country had got on the wrong tack, and the public never knew the real rights of the matter." [1]

Thus we see that while we plead in many departments for more public administration of Industry, it will be very necessary at the same time to guard against the great dangers of officialism and Bureaucracy. We may of course hope that a new alertness in the masses and a far more thorough general education in Citizenship will in the future come to our aid ; but we see that to guard against these dangers *will* require all our alertness.

In the following chapters, however, I have endeavoured to indicate some directions of future movement along which there will be a good hope of passing by in safety, and gaining the haven of a fair and rational social harmony.

[1] See *My Days and Dreams*, p. 262.

INDUSTRY AS AN ART

MR. BERTRAND RUSSELL in his excellent book on *The Principles of Social Reconstruction* accentuates strongly the fact that men's impulses may be divided into two great classes—the Possessive and the Creative—and suggests indeed that the Western nations are even now preparing for a period of transition, in which the possessive instinct will cease to be so influential as it has been in the past, and will begin to yield place to the creative. Let us hope that this change is really taking place. The possessive desires, as Mr. Russell points out, are those which commonly bring people into conflict with one another, and make for warfare on a big or a small scale ; the constructive impulses, on the other hand, are those which on the whole tend towards co-operation and harmony.

That a period of profound and wide-reaching Change is already upon us is a thing to which a thousand indications point ; and it is well that at such a juncture we should pause and peer forward, as best we may, into the future. In the foregoing paper (Ch. II) I have sketched the

Industrial transformation which has been going on during the last fifty or sixty years and the slow modifications of our Capitalist system which have been forced upon us from point to point by the glaring and obvious defects of the latter ; but I confess that for myself I can see nothing *really* adequate and satisfactory in this direction except a complete change of Heart a change of the very guiding principles of our modern life. A mere tinkering at our existing industrial arrangements will never do what we want ; and now that the War has brought us face to face with some of the facts of life and given people furiously to think in a way that they have never done before, the need of a radical Change stands out more clearly before us, and the realisation of such a thing seems less distant and a good deal more feasible.

Are we approaching (I hardly dare ask the question) an age of *good sense* in the affairs of mankind? Is the long-deferred Coming-of-Age of Humanity at last to be celebrated? Let us not pray the gods for any stupendous gifts for the coming generations for towering genius or intellect or universal heroic character but only for a modest boon, such as they surely cannot grudge or refuse to grant to be able, namely, to conduct our own affairs with a little *good sense*, just a very little, as much for instance as a *sheep* might have !

Here we are, the human race, planked down

upon this planet with (at the present day) most marvelous powers of industrial production at our command, amply sufficient, if decently used, to supply every one with all the necessaries of life— and only requiring a very moderate degree of intelligence so to make use of them ; [1] and lo ! instead of settling down to make the best of so excellent a situation we deliberately leave nine-tenths of our brothers and sisters to live in squalid and abject poverty, while the rest of us employ our precious time and energies in mad and destructive warfare !

We have got to get down to the root, and to begin again, so to speak, from the beginning. We have got, it seems to me, to realise two things : first, that Life itself can be made and has to be made something good and beautiful —worth living for, in fact ; secondly, that work itself must be so transformed as to become a pleasure. I will discuss these two points more at length presently. Sufficient just now to observe that the second point necessarily follows from the first. For since work occupies, and

---

[1] As to the necessity of confining (by birth control) our own growing populations—and those of other civilised nations— within reasonable limits, there can hardly be two opinions on its importance. It is so obvious that a well-grown, healthy, and highly developed people is happier in itself and, even though limited in numbers, better able to resist attack than a puny ill-grown horde spawning in ignorance and confusion. See on this subject Havelock Ellis' excellent *Wartime Essays* (Constable, 1916).

must always occupy, the major part of our waking hours, it is clear that our lives generally cannot well be a joy to us if our work is a burden and detestable. And if to some people these two objects of our future endeavor seem *too* remote and impossible, let us remember that since the experience of the Great War *nothing* need seem to us impossible, and that here in these two directions we have a thing indeed worth working for—something even worth giving our lives for—such as we have never had before in all the days of our boasted modern Civilisation.

One serious obstacle to the amelioration indicated, is what Mr. Russell terms the ' Possessive ' impulse—chiefly exhibited among the Well-to-do ; and it may be worth while to say a few words on this. Through long centuries this impulse has been cultivated and evolved, and to such a degree that it has become in many cases a mere mania—the " mania of owning things "—without rhyme or reason. In pursuance of this mania vast numbers of people not only make miserable their own lives (which would not so much matter), but also the lives of thousands around them, from whom they derive their ill-gotten gains. (Even sheep are not so senseless as this.) It is the possessive or grabbing mania which stands in the way of our human approach to the new world that awaits us. Let us hope that the power and vitality of this delusion are fading away, and that soon it will be but a ghost and a bogey through which we shall walk, and find that it has no substance.

The other serious obstacle is the Timidity and want of self-reliance of the mass-peoples in almost all countries ; who—though their hearts, so to speak, are in the right place—have not thought out the logical issue of their feelings and have not in consequence the courage of their opinions. Though there is ample evidence that among all peoples, in some early or pre-civilisation period, life has appeared as worth living, and work as something attractive and enjoyable, yet there is no doubt that in the later centuries the conditions of industry have ingrained into men's minds an opposite view. If any enthusiast to-day were to descend into one of our big towns and, standing at a street corner, to preach to the passers by about the " pleasure of Work," or to urge them to the easy task of making Life " really enjoyable and beautiful," the crowd I fear, putting their thumbs to their noses, would break out in scornful laughter, or perchance turning on the speaker would stone him with stones—even as they stoned Stephen at Jerusalem when for him the heavens opened and he saw in a vision the Son of man standing at the right hand of God.

The truth is that Life and Work to-day under the commercial-industrial regime have become so hideous and monotonous and altogether detestable that to the plain man the very notion of their possible charm and beauty has become ludicrous, and not to be entertained. Nevertheless there are plentiful indications that this hideousness and hatefulness has already reached its climax, and that a new order of world-history is setting in. It is naturally difficult for the mass-people to believe in such a divine possibility of change ; yet I most certainly think that if they once beheld the vision and realised what it meant, they would set their faces towards it in real earnest, and would say in the words of William Blake : " I will not cease from Mental Fight, nor shall my Sword sleep in my hand, till we have built Jerusalem in England's green and pleasant Land."

What then are the necessary conditions for making Work a pleasure?—They are so extraordinarily simple that it is a marvel that they have so far escaped attention and been neglected. Work is a pleasure when it is *free* and *creative* in character—and that is the whole mystery of the matter. There is little else to be said. Every human being, like every animal or plant or tree, has a law of growth of its own, whose expression and utterance is a joy to it. One tree bears oranges, another bears roses. The joy that any such healthy tree has in its work is evident. But only on condition that it is *free,* to produce according to its nature. To try to compel a rose-tree to bear oranges would be madness—a madness similar to that which prevails at present in the whole of our industrial world. So great is the pleasure of free creative work that thousands and hundreds of thousands of folk—as is well known—after their day of leaden and slave-like labor in the factories, do actually on their return home plunge into some sort of hobby of their own—whether gardening, or cabinet-work, leatherwork, copper-embossing, painting, or what not. Tired as they are they still are drawn onwards by the desire to express themselves, to create something of their own ; nor do fresh fatigues deter them from this joyful quest. I know a boy who slaves in a dirty workshop for ten hours or so a day. When he gets home—and a very poor home at that—he actually, after he has had his tea, descends into the *cellar* and by the dim light of a tallow candle and with poor tools begins work again, making little cabinets or corner-cupboards, or a model of an aeroplane. Such people are true artists ; and *all* work of course ought to be of a similar nature—that is, of the nature of an Art.

Artists, in the wide sense of the word, are the only natural and healthy people, and in line with the rest of creation—with the trees and the animals. They are indeed happy. But to confine the name to those who dabble in paints or letters or music is foolish. For the greatest of arts are the arts of Life ; and the washer-woman who takes a real pride and interest in her work, to make it as perfect as she can, independently of any so - called profit or gain which she may derive from it, is an artist in her way, and indeed more truly so in the essence of things than many a man who merely paints pot-boilers for the Spring exhibitions.

Every one ought to be an artist and to take pleasure in his or her work, feeling that the work was a true self-expression and self-liberation. Then there would be joy over the land. (Is the song of a lark work, or is it play?) If Production became free then nearly every one would work in that spirit. And in order that production *should* become free the conditions are also extraordinarily simple—the only condition being that people generally should *desire* it to be free.

Such an Ideal has by statesmen for some centuries never been put into practical shape, or even apparently contemplated with that end in view. Yet one would say that its realisation in a sensible community would not be a very difficult matter. All that would be required would be that every person or group of persons who desired it should have access (at a State or community rent) to a small plot of land on which to establish his or their industry, and access also, under similar conditions, to such power, in the form of electricity or steam or water, as the community could provide. I say " or group of persons " because it is clear that for many industries the work of a group is more appropriate and effective than the work of isolated individuals, and such spontaneously co-operative work (provided the group were self-governing and not enslaved to any master) would be free in character and would carry with it for each worker the charm of authenticity and of being (through the group) the expression of each worker's will. Thus it would be truly artistic, and truly a source of pleasure—being both creative and free. Something of such conditions was certainly realised in the best days of the mediæval guilds. Where on the other hand it happened that the industry was carried on by a single individual, its self - expressional and artistic character would probably be enhanced—though something no doubt might be lost on the social side, and in the pleasure of co-operation.

As I say, there does not seem to be any serious reason why a scheme of this kind (in more adequate detail) should not be worked out, *provided the nation desired it*. The real obstacle —both to the spread of any such Ideal, and to the practical working of it out—lies in the matter we have mentioned above, the excess of ' possessive instinct which pervades large classes. The very extensive and wealthy classes who to-day control production and derive their riches from the enslavement of labor, dread above all things the *freeing* of the worker and the prospect of the latter becoming self-determining and master of his fate. Though it is notorious that the present dispensation produces a rather futile,

mean, and miserable master-class, together with
a dismal, weary, and sad-eyed worker class, yet
the whole political and social engine is concen-
trated on the effort to maintain it as it is, and
to disguise or conceal its evil character. The
lifting of this coffin-lid would be the signal of
a Resurrection such as the world has hardly yet
dreamed of.

A second result would follow from the freeing
of the worker. Not only would Work, being
authentic and creative, become a joy and a bless-
ing ; but the things created would (at any rate
after a brief period of adaptation to the new order)
take on the quality of *Beauty*. The world would
be irradiated with a new light. The things
produced and sold or exchanged in the markets
and the shops, having been made in joy and
gladness, and having absorbed into themselves
the spirit of those who produced them, would
actually radiate back the same spirit on the pur-
chasers and users—not otherwise than as the
luminous paint with which we paint our clock-
dials, after having been exposed to the sunlight
during the day, radiates back a fairy gleam of
the same in the watches of the night. The
wares in the windows, the objects round us in
our rooms, would reflect the conditions of their
production. *They do so now;* and that is
part of the terror, in the present day, of walking
through the streets ! The abject aimless articles
that we see exposed there for sale are the sorry

reflection of the kind of life the mass of our people lead.

The degree to which Beauty, with the inspiration which it affords, is absent from the surroundings of our modern life is a thing which—though it has been dwelt on by a few Artists and Socialists, like Ruskin and William Morris—has generally passed unnoticed by the multitude. Beauty has in truth been so far exiled from our current Works and Days that we have lost the sense of it ; and of that which we have never experienced we have naturally ceased to feel the need. I propose in the following chapter to explain more in detail what this loss is and what it means.

NOTE

It is sometimes said, and even strenuously maintained, that with due regimentation and officialism such as to-day we see existing and extending all around us—with a thoroughgoing system of servile labor, in fact—more and better articles could be and would be produced, than by any such free creative method as above proposed. Personally I very much doubt this assertion. The " more " is just possibly, though not certainly, true ; but the " better " I think is assuredly false—unless, indeed, explosive shells and big guns are to be adopted as the measure of goodness. However, allowing for the moment that the argument is feasible, what does it really at most amount to ? It amounts to this—that cheap and serviceable wares are the main object of life, and that if these are produced it really does not matter about the welfare of the Producers, or whether *their* souls are liberated to a nobler and more human utterance. It is indeed the final conclusion and condemnation of the " Nation of Shopkeepers " theory—and there I think we may leave it !

IV

BEAUTY IN EVERYDAY LIFE [1]

IT is difficult sometimes to make clear what exactly one means by Beauty in daily life. Perhaps one can best attack the subject by pointing out first what one does *not* mean. Not long ago, in walking over the hills on my way to Sheffield, I saw a sight which, alas ! is far from uncommon. I saw one of those charming wayside wells or fountains, which I remembered was gracious, years ago, with sparkling pure water and overhanging ferns and mosses—I saw it neglected and shattered, dried up, and its place filled with broken pots and pans and old salmon tins. The sight afflicted me and, remembering how this was only one instance out of many, I could not help thinking :—Is the love of beauty and the sense of the sacredness of Life and Nature lost to this people? It is impossible (I thought) to imagine the Greeks of old permitting such a crime. They would have slain the man who perpetrated it. For, for them, deities and spirits dwelt in the streams and foun-

[1] Being the substance of a Lecture delivered in Sheffield and elsewhere.

tains, and in the woods and all the sylvan world, and to defile these things was an act of sacrilege. And even our own forefathers, a few centuries ago, had their well - dressings and festivals of gratitude to the gods for all creatures of beauty and use. But we—we have lost the sense of divinity in Nature and Life, and instead, when we ask what is holy and what is sacred, we are pointed to some stuffy chapel or church, with greasy pews and ill-smelling hymn-books, and ever-closed windows—and told that *there* we must doff our hats and speak with bated breath ! Not that I have anything to say against churches and chapels—for those who like them ; but I do think it sad that all our reverence should be piled upon these things to the neglect of those others ; and that while we sing our hymns to God on the Sundays we should employ the rest of the week in emptying our slops in the streams and pouring foul volumes of smoke up into the glorious and crystal vault of heaven. I can hardly believe that God likes that sort of worship !

And it is not only Nature that is thus desecrated, but that Man himself, who ought to be the crown and pride of Nature, has become a blot upon her face. The other day I was passing in the train along the coast not far from the shore. It was a Spring day ; the sun shone brightly ; before me was a field in which men were plowing and beyond it stretched the sea.

It was a beautiful scene—the sky above, flecked with fleecy clouds, the darker blue, foam-broken waves, the rich brown of the land ; the white birds (sea-gulls) following in the furrow ; the splendid well-equipped horses. All (I was going to say) was full of life and promise.—And then I looked at the men ! and saw with sorrow two ill-dressed, poverty-stricken, poorly-built, and obviously weary " farmhands " trudging there behind their teams—the one note of sadness and disharmony in the scene. Why should this be? They say that in China at the Spring Equinox, it has been the custom of centuries for the Emperor to go forth with a silver plow and plow a few furrows in ceremonial state—this in token of the honor attaching to so important a work—an honor so great that even an Emperor may covet to stand thus " as Mediator between Earth and Heaven." Can we in the end of time devise nothing better or more worthy than *our* method? The work of the plowman, in all pagan times and since the dawn of History has been honored. Why should it not be so now?

And if there is a Festival which in the Old World has been celebrated with dance and with song, more even than the Spring-sowings, it has been the garnering and the threshing of the corn. To-day, what do I see when this period comes round? I declare that I fairly dread its arrival ! I hear a horrible rumbling ill-omened

sound. I look forth ; and behold a foul and
dirty and splay-jointed engine creaking along
the road, belching forth clouds of filthy smoke,
and followed by a threshing machine and a dozen
or so of the most god-forsaken, wretched men
who have been picked up for next to nothing
among the 'unemployed.' This Machine and
this crew pass into a farmyard, there to perform
their horrid rites, and through the belly of the
former and the hands of the latter passes the
beautiful corn, in a fashion so inhuman that
I cannot help wondering whether, after the process, the grain is fit to be eaten.

And when we leave the fields and pass into
the factories—away from the redeeming influences
of the open air—the case, as we all know, is
worse. Where in the long drab rooms, filled with
drab-coloured men and women and children, in
the stifling air, and amid the clatter of machinery
and the wicked scream of wheels,—where are
the most beggarly elements of beauty and of
joy in life? Alas ! they are not to be found.
Commercialism says they do not *pay* ; and
Puritanism, her handmaid, has declared them
to be *wicked*. On one occasion, at Kilbowie,
near Glasgow, I stood on the bridge (not at
midnight but at midday) at the hour when
Singer's great sewing-machine factory is loosed
for its dinner time. A human torrent—some *ten
thousand* men and girls as it was then reckoned
—passed rapidly over. And I, ensconced in a

sheltered corner, stood and looked at their faces. It was not necessary for me to go inside. Standing there I could see only too clearly the conditions which prevailed within the factory (no worse probably than elsewhere in the Kingdom) ; they were written on the listless tired faces, the lightless eyes, the monotone expressions, the pallid skins, the peaked features, the perkily sexual physiognomies. I came away feeling depressed indeed.

When living at Brighton as a boy, more than fifty years ago, I used to hear of the miners in the North whose coal—often brought in sea-borne ships to the neighboring little harbor of Shoreham—we were in the habit of burning. And I used to think what grand fellows those miners must be, who faced danger and death in the pits, and heavy toil, in order to obtain this so necessary fuel—what strong and well-grown men, and honored by the nation, as of course they ought to be. Fate or destiny have led me, in these later years, to live within three or four miles of the coal pits of North-East Derbyshire ; and now I know the miners of that locality well. Sometimes it happens to me to be in the station at Chesterfield when the " Paddy Mail " comes in—the train which brings the men back from the outlying pits. I shall never forget the moment when first I watched the arrival of this train. Instead of the fine hearty fellows my boyish imagination had pictured, there descended from the overcrowded carriages and hurried away across the platform as if ashamed of themselves a shambling ragged crew, whose thin legs and worn features spoke only too clearly of want and overwork. Of course there were some sturdy and comfortable specimens among the crowd, but they were the exception. Rickety limbs, contracted chests, hacking coughs and hollow cheeks, abounded ; and now, with more intimate knowledge of the subject, I am conscious that that first impression was very near the mark   Somehow, despite occasional bursts of good times and good luck, these men who do some of society's most needed work are left, through ignorance, neglect, and oppression, to become its bitter enemies. And one can only ask, Where are the splendors and the joys of life which should be their portion?

Finally when we follow the workers—of either sex—from the factories and furnaces and shops to their own homes, what do we find? Every one unfortunately knows something of the miles of mean streets in our great towns, which, as John Burns once said, "make mean men, weary women and unclean children." What elements are there in these surroundings, to feed the soul and give it nourishment? What stimulus to save it from the deadly pall of monotony? Those who are sufficiently well off to command frequent change do not know how paralysing is the effect of monotony ; but those who have had the good

5

fortune to be confined in prison for a long period, or have been compelled to work in a factory, do. On one occasion, some manual worker friends of mine, man and wife, who resided normally in a small country cottage, took their two children for a little holiday to the seaside. They let down at a lodging there—a house in a row, of the usual type ; and while they were unpacking their few belongings they told the children to run out and play in the street. The children did so, and for some minutes all went well. Then suddenly heartrending screams were heard. The parents rushed to the window, thinking the kiddies had, by chance, been run over. But no, nothing of the kind. There were the boy and girl safe and sound, but crying their little hearts out in a paroxysm of despair. What was the matter? They had run a little way along the street, and lo ! there they were staring up at the senseless row of tall houses in front of them, *all exactly alike*, of which it was impossible to tell *which* was the one whence they had lately emerged, and where their parents would be found. It was a veritable nightmare—this row of grinning idiotic house-fronts all exactly the same, down to the very lace-curtains—and a nightmare which they would never forget to the end of their days.

I tell this story in order to illustrate the sad, the paralysing effect of uniformity and monotony in the present day lives of our mass-peoples,

both children and adults. I think anyhow I
have said sufficient to indicate—by illustrations
drawn from their *absence*—what I mean by the
need and the importance in our industrial world,
of the positive things—of Health and Joy and
Love and Beauty—the things without which our
mortal days on Earth are of little or no account.
And I think I now begin to understand why
to thousands, and one may say millions, this
War (even with all its horrors) has been a relief
and an escape, why it has brought alertness of
mind and brightness of eyes with it.   And
the answer is :—Because—dreadful and wicked
though it be—it has meant to so many a
life in the open-air ; it has meant health, good
food, a common cause, comradeship with others,
and a dozen positive things, instead of the
inhuman monotonies and negations of a life of
slave labour under the heel of commercialism.
I understand that wicked as the War is, it is in
its essence the outcome and result of something
more wicked ; and I pray that when afterwards
the millions return to their homes they will see
to it that never again shall the soulless regime
of the past be reinstated, but that industrial life
shall go forward into a new länd—the land of
freedom and of joy.

There is one thing which the War has done
in which we are all agreed. It has convinced
us that it will be no use in the future pleading
Poverty as our excuse for the continuance of

the past conditions.   This People of ours, which
has been able to rise up and pour out money
like water for the purposes of the present conflict,
can never again say that resources are wanting
for the far more important purpose of creating
for itself a really worthy and great national life.
We have indeed discovered the amazing extent
of our industrial wealth, and its amazing growth.
In 1830, as already said (Ch. I.), the combined
value of our Imports and Exports amounted to
£88,000,000 ; shortly before the War this had
risen to £1,000,000,000.   The National Income
at the same time reached £2,000,000,000.   Yet
during that period—when individual merchants and
manufacturers were making enormous fortunes—
it was commonly said that such things as old-
age pensions, shorter working days, free meals
for children and so forth, were too expensive
to be contemplated.   We know now what these
excuses amounted to.

We are beginning to understand too the false-
ness of the plea, sometimes put forward, that the
mass-peoples are indifferent to such things as
Health, Freedom, and the real joy of creative
industry, and are quite content as long as they
have their bread and butter, and their few
trumpery amusements.   It is certain (as I have
noted in the previous chapter) that the creative
instinct and the feeling for beauty are widespread
and deeply rooted in the hearts of the people,
and that in all times and lands the peasants and

the craft workers in their potteries, or wrought
iron-work, or textile fabrics, have—when left with
a little independence to their own devices—felt
and found their way to results quite admirable and
beautiful. Why is it that great artists like Ruskin
and Morris and Walter Crane have for long
enough pointed this out to unheeding generations,
and that travelers going to out of the way places
and the ends of the earth have brought us back
countless specimens of such native talent? Lately,
at the Exhibition of the Design and Industries
Association, held in London (November 1916),
there were shown some colored cotton cloths
copied from designs made by the native tribes
of West Africa in connexion with their hand-
loom industry ; and certainly the beauty of these
things, the richness of the colors and the excel-
lence of the fabrics, were an eye-opener to those
who thought that on such matters Manchester and
South Kensington had said the last word.   The
truth is that the love of beauty is natural among
all free peoples—though of course its standard
may vary in quality and character ; and we may
well believe that some aboriginal folk living in
the open air and the light of the African sun have
an acuter sense of color and form than many of
our populations who are surrounded by the
monotonous and drab conditions of which I have
spoken.

Mr. Chester Holcombe, for some time Acting
Minister of the United States at Peking, says

of the Chinese people [1] :— They have a keenly
sensitive æsthetic taste. Evidences of this fact
are to be found in every direction and among
all classes throughout the empire. . . . Their love
of the odd and grotesque, in imitation or variation of nature, is more apparent than real, and
is mainly shown in dwarf copies of natural objects
of grandeur or beauty. This is the result of
necessity rather than of choice, and should be
credited to a hunger for the beautiful, so keen
that in the absence of the originals they can find
pleasure in the merest toy-copies. Hence all over
China, in the homes of the poorest as well as of
the wealthy, in door-yards and dwellings, are
to be found tiny landscapes, dwarf trees, mimic
caves and grottos, artificial rockwork, and mountains of a few feet in height, threads of running
water, or lakes that a child might spring across.
All this is the struggle of poverty to surround
and satisfy itself with the beautiful. And as
such it has a right to recognition and respect. . . .
Throughout the empire," he goes on to say, " hill-
slopes, mountain-crags, and similar points com-
manding a wide range of vision, were chosen
centuries ago as sites for their temples, pagodas,
and other sacred and important edifices. The
writer stood one autumn day by a ruined building
placed upon the highest point in the Imperial
Summer Palace, west of Peking. On every hand,

[1] See *The Real Chinaman*, by Chester Holçombe (Hodder &
Stoughton, 1895).

marring what must once have been a scene of exquisite beauty, were blackened, broken and roofless walls, and other marks of the desolation wrought by British and French troops when they plundered and burned this palace in 1860. Where the writer stood were to be seen a few Chinese characters recently written upon one of the posts of a finely wrought but broken gateway, Translated, they read as follows :—' A *gentleman* would not so far demean himself as to consent to the mutilation and destruction of this wonderfully beautiful landscape. "

I think we must admit that the Chinese citizen who scrawled this on the broken gate-post had not only a fine sense of beauty but also a keen faculty for polite yet searching rebuke.

The truth is that the germ of the Beauty-sense is slumbering in the hearts of all peoples, not only in the Chinese or Japanese peasants whose productions we admire, but even in our more solid and stolid British stocks. But it is very commonly starved out on the one hand by sheer poverty or paralysed on the other by mere superfluity of wealth.

I have spoken in the preceding chapter of the charm of the technique of the mediæval guilds, as seen in their architecture and other craft-work, and suggested how much of the charm derives from the freedom and spontaneity and authenticity of these productions. I do not think we yet perceive what a large element in the consciousness of Beauty is our recognition of a *personal* factor behind it. I mean that the sense that here is an intelligence seeking for expression adds greatly to our appreciation of the beautiful. It is not every thing of course, but it is an important element—and one that has not been sufficiently considered by the professors and the schools. A rose is presented to you, whose color and form appear perfect ; a living creature, it seems, unfolding its life to the world—in some way striving to express itself. But when suddenly you discover that the flower is an artificial one, what a sense of loss supervenes ! Certain elements of beauty remain, it is true, but one most important element—the consciousness of touch upon a kindred life—is gone.

This is so far true that I think it largely explains the *ugliness* of machine-made things. Here is a row of iron railings. From the South Kensington point of view it may be a very desirable row. The design of each shaft and of the scroll which connects it with the adjacent shaft may be excellent ; but when a thousand such shafts and scrolls appear in regimental monotony the mind is paralysed ; there is no sense of expressiveness or of personality, only a sense of weary repetition ; and one great factor of beauty is lost. So it comes about that, though one may look at a single artificial rose or wrought-iron scroll with pleasure and in admiration of the ingenuity and skill of the artificer, one turns away from the thousand mechanical copies in disgust.

To be quite practical. Though one can see that there may be not a few intermediate stages to be passed through before this ideal of Industry as an Art can be realised, yet one can see that to keep one's eye fixed on that ideal is the best way of arriving there. The mechanical organisation of Industry may have to be retained for a period, but it must be retained only with a view to the liberation beneath it of the human spirit and of human creativeness. A purely mechanical industry may be retained long in some trades—like the weaving of cotton sheeting or the turning out of steel rails (where uniformity is the main thing required)—longer than in other trades where the human impress is more important. But in such cases the actual length of hours worked under machine-conditions might be so reduced that each employee still had the major part of the day for his own personal and authentic activity. A four hours' shift in many trades would be quite feasible ; and practically no worker would object to giving this amount of time provided he had the rest of the day free for the industry in which he was really interested.

As said before, a Wealth which exists only for the purpose of producing *more* Wealth is the most foolish and futile thing imaginable. It is worse—it is poisonous and disease-producing.

For a hundred years now, in this and other Western countries, this Dispensation has lasted ; and it has resulted (as many of us foretold years ago) in the deposit of a mass of mere dregs in the bottom of the social chalice, and the spread of a quite foul scum on the top. Possibly nothing but the strain and suffering of a great War could avail to purge the body politic of these evils. We have given endless thought and labor to the perfecting of breeds of Cattle and Cabbages and to the awarding of prizes for the same in countless shows and exhibitions ; but we have only thought of the men and women themselves as machines for the grinding out of profit. And now the Nemesis is on us.

Let me recount, in illustration of my meaning, what happened in Manchester three or four years ago. The old Infirmary had been pulled down, leaving a large open space at the end of Market Street, and nearly in the centre of the city. The question naturally arose, What should be done with this open space? and the idea was widely favoured to convert it into an ornamental garden, with plentiful seats and resting-places for the busy public. At a meeting of the City Council a resolution to that effect was proposed, and seemed likely to be carried—when a Councillor got up and said " No—no, you cannot do this ; for if you plant an ornamental garden there with seats, what will be the consequence? Why, all the dirty, unclean, poverty-stricken loafers that you see about the streets now will flock there, and after them it will be impossible for any clean and self-respecting citizen to use the place—so *that* plan had better be abandoned." After the Councillor had spoken there was a dead silence in the Council. It was seen that no reply was possible, and that the scheme would *have* to be abandoned. As a matter of fact I have known almost identical things happen in other Northern towns, and schemes for their improvement similarly paralysed.

We need a new gospel of Wealth—namely the liberation of the *real* wealth of this and other nations—the up-building of a glad and free creative Life among the millions, and the growth of a healthy, alert, handsome, and capable population, having in their midst the priceless flower of beauty, and faithfully tending it in their daily life.

V

NON-GOVERNMENTAL SOCIETY

MOST people agree nowadays in the view (to which I have alluded already) that the growth of bureaucracy and officialism in the modern State is a serious evil, and that the extension of Government interference and the multiplication of Laws are a great danger. We all know that the institution of the Law and the Courts actually creates and gives rise to huge masses of evil—bribery, blackmail, perjury, spying and lying, wrongful accusation, useless and deliberate suffering and cruelty ; that it publicly sanctions and organises violence, even in extreme forms ; that it quite directly and deliberately supports vast and obvious wrongs in Society—as for instance land-monopoly ; that it is absurd and self-contradictory in much of its theory and practice ; that (as Herbert Spencer so frequently insists) it paralyses the folk that submit or trust to it ; and finally that it is to-day for the most part so antiquated and out of date that (even if this were thought desirable) it might well seem impracticable to patch it up for real human use.

Yet in these cases—though we admit that the

things are evil—our defence usually is that they carry some compensations with them, and that anyhow they are *necessary* evils, which we cannot dispense with, and without which disorder, violence and social disruption would ensue.

It may be worth while to consider this defence more closely ; for curiously enough the history of nations and peoples is, on the whole, to contrary effect. Not only have all the early tribes of the world got on and cohered together in order and social amity without any rigid and ponderous system of laws ; but even among the peasant peoples of to-day—like the Irish or the Swedes or the Swiss or the Chinese—where they are still living in moderately primitive conditions, we find the same thing. Governmental law and its operations and institutions occupy but a very small part in their lives. It is true that Custom is strong among all primitive folk, no doubt as a very necessary backbone or framework to their society ; but Custom is a very different thing from Law. It is law in its inception—when it is yet in a tentative, rudimentary condition ; and however harsh, rigid, or senseless the customs of many savage tribes may be, they are yet easier to alter than when they have become ossified into written forms, with their huge weight of age and ceremony, and the authority of armed men to enforce them.[1]

[1] *See* below, p. 90. Spencer and Gillen, in their late book *The Northern Tribes of Australia*, say that there are no chiefs

That human societies can subsist without a considerable amount of Custom we may well doubt ; but that they can subsist and maintain themselves in good order and vitality without written law and its institutions there is no reason at all to doubt. And when Custom, among a reasonable and moderately advanced people, leaving behind the barbarities of the savage age, takes on a gentler form, and while exercising considerable pressure on individuals is itself fairly plastic and adaptable to the general movements of society—we seem to see in such pressure a force as far superior to Law as life itself is superior to mere mechanism. A vast amount of our social life to-day in all departments of its activity is ruled by Custom, and some of these customs, like those of " society " and fashion, have a very powerful sway. There is no *law*, for instance, for the recovery of betting debts, yet their non-payment is extremely rare.

Of course, accustomed as we are to " call the policeman " on every emergency, we find it hard to imagine life without this institution ; and our life being largely founded on it, it *is* so far necessary, and its removal would cause dislocation. That is, since without the police the present spoliation of the poor would not be possible,

even or headmen among these people ; but the old men constitute an informal council, which punishes " crime " and the breaking of marriage rules, organises the ceremonies, and from time to time inaugurates reforms.

and the enormous existing inequalities of wealth and poverty could never have been heaped up —without them the society founded on these artificial inequalities could not well be maintained.[1] But to say that because a certain institution is necessary to build up and retain society in a certain abnormal and unnatural form, therefore society cannot exist without that institution, is the same as to say that because to a Chinese woman of rank foot-bandages are necessary, therefore women generally cannot exist without foot-bandages. We have to realise that our present social forms are as ugly and inhuman as a club foot ; and then we shall begin to realise how little necessary are these institutions, like law and police, whose chief concern and office is to retain and defend these forms.

The chief difficulty, then, which arises in people's minds at the thought of a free non-governmental society does not concern its desirability—they are agreed as a rule that it would be desirable—but concerns its practicability. And much of this difficulty is derived from the society of the present. People see, in fact, that an internecine competition for subsistence is the ruling force of life to-day, and the chief incentive to production, and they infer that without government society would dissolve

[1] Though, as all more primitive society shows us, small inequalities and such as arise from natural differences of human industry and capacity will always be welcome.

into a mere chaos of plunder on the one hand, and of laziness on the other.[1] It is this difficulty which has first to be removed.

Though it seems a hard thing to say, the outer life of society to-day is animated first and foremost by Fear. From the wretched wage-slave, who rises before the break of day, hurries through squalid streets to the dismal sound of the "hummer," engages for nine, ten, or twelve hours, and for a pittance wage, in monotonous work which affords him no interest, no pleasure ; who returns home to find his children gone to bed, has his supper, and, worn out and weary, soon retires himself, only to rise again in the morning and pursue the same deadly round ; and who leads a life thus monotonous, inhuman, and devoid of all dignity and reality, simply because he is hounded to it by the dread of starvation ;— to the big commercial man, who, knowing that his wealth has come to him through speculation and the turns and twists of the market, fears that it may at any moment take to itself wings by the same means ; who feels that the more wealth he has, the more ways there are in which he may lose it, the more cares and anxieties belonging to it ; and who to continually make his position secure is, or thinks himself, forced to stoop to all sorts of mean and dirty tricks ;—

---

[1] Though it must, to be strictly impartial, be pointed out that this difficulty is chiefly felt by those classes who themselves live on interest and in ornamental idleness.

over the great mass of people the same demon spreads its dusky wings. Feverish anxiety is the keynote of their lives. There is no room for natural gladness or buoyancy of spirits. You may walk the streets of our great cities, but you will hear no one singing—except for coppers ; hardly a plowboy to-day whistles in the furrow, and in almost every factory (this is a fact) if a workman sang at his work he would be " sacked." We are like shipwrecked folk clambering up a cliff. The waves are raging below. Each one clings by handhold or foothold where he may, and in the panic if he push his neighbor from a point of vantage, it is to be regretted certainly, but it cannot be helped.

But such a state of affairs is not normal. Allowing that the struggle for existence in some degree or form is unavoidable, history still, except at rare crises, presents us with no such spectacle of widespread anxiety ; the study of native races —whom *we* might consider in a state of destitution—reveals no such dominion of dread. I want the reader to imagine for a moment this burden of fear lifted off the hearts of a whole people ; and the result.

Let us imagine for a moment that some good fairy—some transcendental Chancellor of the Exchequer—with a stroke of his wand, has assured to us all not only an old age pension, but a decent provision for all our days of the actual necessaries of life (to go no further than that) ;

6

so that for the future no man could feel any serious or grinding anxiety for his own material safety, or that of his family. What would be the result on our actions?

Perhaps, as many would maintain, nine-tenths of the population would say, "I'm blessed if I'll ever do another stroke of work." Like the organ-grinder who came into a little fortune, and who forthwith picked up an axe and fell upon his organ, shouting as he hacked it to pieces, "You shall neffer play dat tam *Alabama Coon* any more," we should feel so sick of our present jobs that we should want to turn our backs on them for ever. Very likely, I should say—and rightly enough too ; for "work" in the present day is done under such degrading and miserable conditions by the vast majority of the population that the very best and most manly thing would be to refuse to continue doing it.

But let us suppose, since a bare living has been assured to us, and we are in no danger of actual starvation, that we all take a good long holiday, and abstain religiously from doing anything. Suppose that we simply twirl our thumbs in idleness for two, three, four, or six months. Still, is it not obvious that at the end of that time nine-tenths of the population would find sheer idleness appallingly dreary, and that they would *set themselves* to work at some thing or other—to produce comforts or conveniences rising above the level of sheer necessity—objects of use or beauty, either for themselves, or for their families and neighbors, or even conceivably for society at large ; that, in fact, a spontaneous and free production of goods would spring up, followed of course by a spontaneous and free exchange—a self-supporting society, based not on individual dread and anxiety, but on the common fulness of life and energy?

That people relieved from care do spontaneously set themselves to work is sufficiently shown by the case of the well-to-do classes today. For these people, though having *everything* provided for them, and not merely the bare necessaries which we have supposed, exhibit the most extraordinary and feverish energy in seeking employment. A few decades of years have been quite sufficient to make them feel the utter failure of picnics as an object in life ; and now we are flooded with philanthropic and benevolent societies, leagues, charity organisations, art missions to the poor, vigilance crusades, and other activities, which are simply the expression of the natural energies of the human being seeking an outlet in social usefulness. It is, of course, to be regretted that owing to the very imperfect education of this class their ideas and their capacities of social usefulness should be so limited. However, this is a defect which will no doubt be remedied in the future. All that concerns us here is to see that since the rich, though in many ways ill-adapted by training and tradition, do spontaneously take up a life of this kind, there is nothing extravagant in supposing that the average man, surrounded by so many unfulfilled needs, might do the same.

And if any one still doubts let him consider the thousands in our large towns to-day who would give their ears to be able to get out and work on the land—not so much from any prospect of making a fortune that way, as from mere love of the life ; or who in their spare time cultivate gardens or plots or allotments as a hobby ; or the thousands who when the regular day's work is over start some fresh little occupation of their own—some cabinet-making, wood-turning, ornamental iron-work or whatnot ; the scores of thousands, in fact, that there are of *natural* gardeners, cabinet-makers, iron-workers, and so forth ; and then think how if they were free these folk would sort themselves spontaneously to the work they delighted in.

Thus it appears to be at least *conceivable* that a people not hounded on by compulsion nor kept in subjection by sheer authority, would set itself spontaneously to produce the things which it prized. It does not, of course, at once follow that the result would be perfect order and harmony. But there are a few considerations in the positive direction which I may introduce here.

In the first place, each person would be guided in the selection of his occupation by his own taste and skill, or at any rate would be guided by these to a greater extent than he is to-day ; and on the whole would be more likely to find the work for which he was fitted than he is now. The increase in effective output and vitality from this cause alone would be great. While the immense *variety* of taste and skill in human beings would lead to a corresponding variety of spontaneous products.

In the second place, the work done would be useful. It is certain that no man would freely set himself to dig a hole, only to fill it up again —though it is equally certain that a vast amount of the work done to-day is no more useful than that. If a man were a cabinet-maker and made a chest of drawers, either for himself or a neighbor, he would make it so that the drawers would open and shut ; but nine-tenths of the chests made on commercial principles are such that the drawers will neither open nor shut. They are not meant to be useful ; they are meant to have the semblance of being useful ; but they are really made to *sell*. To sell, and by selling yield a profit. And for that purpose they are better adapted if, appearing useful, they turn out really useless, for then the buyer must come again, and so yield another profit to the manufacturer and the merchant. The waste to the community to-day arising from causes of this kind is enormous ; but it is of no moment as long as there is profit to a certain class.

Work in a free society would be done because it was useful. It is curious, when you come to think of it, that there is no other conceivable reason why work should be done. And of course I here include what is beautiful under the term useful,—as there is no reason why one should separate what satisfies one human need, like the need of beauty, from another human need, like the need of food. I say the idea of work implies that it is undertaken because the product itself satisfies some human need. But strangely enough in Commerce that is not so. The work is undertaken in order that the product may *sell*, and so yield a profit ; that is all. It is of no moment *what* the product is, or whether bad or good, as long as it fulfils this one condition. And so the whole spirit of life and industry in the other society would be so utterly different from that of the present, that it is really difficult for us to compare the results. But it is not difficult to see that if on the principles of freedom there was not so *much* produced in mere quantity, and folk did not (as may indeed be hoped) work so many hours a day as now, still, the goods turned out being sincere and genuine, there would really be far more value shown in a year than on the strictly commercial system.

In the third place, it follows—as William Morris so constantly maintained—that " work " in the new sense would be a pleasure—one of the greatest pleasures undoubtedly of life ; and this one fact would transform its whole character. We cannot say that now. How many are there who take real pleasure and satisfaction in their daily labor? Are they, in each township, to be counted on the fingers? But what is the good of life if its chief element, and that which must always be its chief element, is odious? No, the only true economy is to arrange so that your daily labor shall be itself a joy. Then, and then only, are you on the safe side of life. And, your work being such, its product is sure to become beautiful ; that painful distinction between the beautiful and the useful dies out, and everything made is an artistic product. Art becomes conterminous with life.

Thus it will be observed that whereas the present society is founded on a law-enforced system of Private Property, in which, almost necessarily, the covetous hard type of man becomes the large proprietor, and (supported by law and government) is enabled to prey upon the small one ; and whereas the result of this arrangement is a bitter and continuous struggle for possession, in which the motive to activity is mainly Fear ; we, on the contrary, are disentangling a conception of a society in which Private Property is supported by no apparatus of armed authority, but as far as it exists is a perfectly spontaneous arrangement, in which the main motives to activity are neither Fear nor greed of Gain, but rather Community of life and Interest in life—in which, in fact, you undertake work because you *like* the work, because you feel that you can do it, and because you know that the product will be useful, either to yourself or some one else !

How Utopian it all sounds ! How absurdly simple and simple-minded—to work because you like the work and desire the product. How delightful if it could be realised, but, of course, how " unpractical " and impossible.

Yet is it really impossible? From Solomon to Dr. Watts we have been advised to go to the Ant and the Bee for instruction, and lo ! they are unpractical and Utopian too. Can anything be more foolish than the conduct of these little creatures, any one of whom will at any moment face death in defence of his tribe? while the Bee is absolutely so ignorant and senseless, that instead of storing up the honey that it has gathered in a little cell of its own, with a nice lock and key, it positively puts it in the common cells, and cannot distinguish it from the stores of the others. Foolish little Bee, the day will surely come when you will bitterly rue your " unthrifty " conduct, and you will find yourself starving while your fellow-tribesmen are consuming the fruits of your labor.

And the human body itself, that marvelous epitome and mirror of the universe, how about that? Is it not Utopian too? It is composed of a myriad cells, members, organs, compacted

into a living unity.   A healthy body is the most
perfect society conceivable.   What does the hand
say when a piece of work is demanded of it?
Does it bargain first for what reward it is to
receive, and refuse to move until it has secured
satisfactory terms, or the foot decline to take
us on a journey till it knows what special gain
is to accrue to *it* thereby?   Not so ; but each
limb and cell does the work which is before it
to do, and (such is the Utopian law) the *fact of
its doing the work* causes the circulation to flow
to it, and it is nourished and fed in proportion
to its service.   And we have to ask whether the
same may not be the law of a healthy human
society?   Whether the fact of a member doing
service (however humble) to the community would
not be quite sufficient to ensure his provision
by the rest with all that he might need?   Whether
the community would think of allowing such an
one to starve any more than a man would think
of allowing his least finger to pine away and
die?   Whether it is not possible that men would
cease to feel any anxiety about the " reward of
their labor " ; that they would think first of
their work and the pleasure they had in doing
it, and would not doubt that the reward would
follow?

For indeed the instinct to do anything which
is obviously before you to do, which is wanted,
and which you *can* do, is very strong in human
nature.   Even children, those rudimentary savages,

are often extremely proud to be " useful," and it is conceivable that we might be sensible enough, instead of urging them as we do now to " get on," to make money, to beat their fellows in the race of life, and by climbing on other folk's heads to ultimately reach a position where they would have to work no longer,—that we might teach them how when they grew up they would find themselves members of a self-respecting society which, while it provided them *gratis* with all they might need, would naturally expect them in honor to render some service in return. Even small children could understand that. Is it quite inconceivable that a society of grown men and women might act up to it?

But it is really absurd to argue about the possibility of these things in human society, when we have so many actual examples of them before our eyes. Herman Melville, in that charming book *Typee*, describes the Marquesas Islanders of the Pacific, among whom he lived for some time during the year 1846. He says: " During the time I lived among the Typees no one was ever put upon his trial for any offence against the public. To all appearances there were no courts of law or equity. There was no municipal police for the purposes of apprehending vagrants or disorderly characters. In short, there were no legal provisions whatever for the well-being and conservation of society, the enlightened end of civilised legislation." Nevertheless, the whole book is a eulogy of the social arrangements he met with, and with almost a fervor of romance in its tone ; and yet, like all his description of the natives of the Pacific Islands, undoubtedly accurate, and well corroborated by the travelers of the period. An easy communism prevailed. When a good haul of fish was made, those who took part in it did not keep the booty to themselves, but parceled it out, and sent it throughout the tribe, retaining only their proportionate share. When one family required a new cabin, the others would come and help to build it. He describes such an occasion, when, "at least a hundred of the natives were bringing materials to the ground, some carrying in their hands one or two of the canes which were to form the sides, others slender rods of hibiscus, strung with palmetto leaves, for the roof. Every one contributed something to the work ; and by the united but easy labors of all the entire work was completed before sunset."

Similar communistic habits prevail, of course, through a vast number of savage tribes, and indeed almost anywhere that the distinctively commercial civilisation has not set its mark. They may be found close at home, as in the little primitive island of St. Kilda, in the Hebrides, where exactly the same customs of sharing the hauls of fish or the labors of housebuilding exist to-day,[1] which Melville describes in *Typee* ; and

---

[1] See Chapter XI of *Poverty and the State*, by H. V. Mills.

they may be found all along the edges of our
civilisation in the harvesting and house-warming
" bees " of the backwoods and outlying farm-
populations. And we may fairly ask, not whether
such social habits are possible, but whether they
are not in the end the only possible form ; for
surely it is useless and absurd to call these modern
hordes of people, struggling with each other for
the means of subsistence, and jammed down by
violent and barbaric penal codes into conditions
which enforce the struggle, *societies* ; as it would
be absurd to call the wretched folk in the Black
Hole of Calcutta a society. If any one will
only think for a minute of his own inner nature
he will see that the only society which would ever
really satisfy him would be one in which he
was perfectly free, and yet bound by ties of
deepest trust to the other members ; and if he
will think for another minute he will see that
the only conditions on which he could be perfectly
free (to do as he liked) would be that he *should*
trust and care for his neighbor as well as himself. The conditions are perfectly simple ; and
since they have been more or less realised by
countless primitive tribes of animals and men,
it is surely not impossible for civilised man to
realise them. If it be argued (which is perfectly
true) that modern societies are so much more
complex than the primitive ones, we may reply
that if modern man, with his science and his
school-boards, and his brain cultivated through

all these centuries, is not competent to solve a more complex problem than the savage, he had better return to savagery.

But it is getting time to be practical.

Of the *possibility* of a free communal society there can really, I take it, be no doubt. The question that more definitely presses on us now is one of transition—by what steps shall we, or can we pass to that land of freedom?

We have supposed a whole people started on its journey by the lifting off of a burden of Fear and anxiety ; but in the long, slow ascent of evolution sudden miraculous changes are not to be expected ; and for this reason alone it is obvious that we can look for no very swift transformation to the communal form. Peoples that have learnt the lesson of " trade " and competition so thoroughly as the modern nations have —each man fighting for his own hand—must take some time to unlearn it. The sentiment of the common life, so long nipped and blighted, must have leisure to grow and expand again ; and we acknowledge that—in order to foster new ideas and new habits—an intermediate stage of definite industrial organisation may be quite necessary.

When one looks sometimes at the awful residue and dregs which were being left as a legacy to the future by our present commercial system— the hopeless, helpless, drunken, incapable men and women who drift through London and the country districts from workhouse to workhouse, or the equally incapable and more futile idlers in high places, one feels that possibly only a rather stringent industrial organisation (such as the War has brought upon us) could have enabled society to cope with these burdens. The hand of the nation has already been forced to the development of Farm-colonies, Land-reclamations, Afforestation, Canal-restoration, and other big industrial schemes, and these are leading to a considerable socialisation of land and machinery. At the same time the rolling up of companies into huge and huger trusts is, as we plainly see, making the transference of industries to public control and to public uses, daily more easy to effect.

On the other hand, the Trade Unions and Co-operative Societies by the development of productive as well as distributive industries, and by the interchange of goods with each other on an ever-growing scale, are bringing about a similar result. They are creating a society in which enormous wealth is produced and handled not for the profit of the few, but for the use of the many ; a *voluntary* collectivism working within and parallel with the official collectivism of the State.

As this double collectivism grows and spreads, profit-grinding will more and more cease to be a lucrative profession. Though no doubt great efforts will be made in the commercial world to discountenance the public organisation of the unemployed (because this will cut away the ground

of cheap labor on which commercialism is built),
yet as we have seen, the necessity of this organisation has reached such a point that it can no
longer be denied. And as it comes in more
and more, it will more and more react on the
conditions of the employed, causing them also to
be improved. Besides, we are fain to hope that
something else of which we see growing signs
on every hand, will also come in—namely a new
sense of social responsibility, a new reading of
religion, a healthier public opinion—which will
help on and give genuine life to the changes
of which we speak. If so, it might not be so
very long before the spread of employment, and
the growing security of decent wages, combined
with the continual improvement of productive pro-
cesses and conditions, would bring about a kind
of general affluence—or at least absence of
poverty. The unworthy fear which haunts the
hearts of nine-tenths of the population, the anxiety
for the beggarly elements of subsistence, would
pass away or fade in the background, and with
it the mad nightmarish competition and bitter
struggle of men with each other. Even the sense
of Property itself would be alleviated. To-day
the institution of Property is like a cast-iron railing
against which a human being may be crushed,
but which still is retained because it saves us
from falling into the gulf. But to-morrow, when
the gulf of poverty is practically gone, the indi-
cating line between one person and another

need run no harsher than an elastic band.[1]
People will wake up with surprise, and rub their
eyes to find that they are under no necessity of
being other than human.

Simultaneously (i.e. with the lessening of the
power of money as an engine of interest and
profit-grinding) the huge nightmare which weighs
on us to-day, the monstrous incubus of " business "
—with its endless Sisyphus labors, its searchings
for markets, its displacement and destruction of
rivals, its travelers, its advertisements, its armies
of clerks, its banking and broking, its accounts
and checking of accounts—will fade and lessen
in importance ; till some day perchance it will
collapse, and roll off like a great burden to the
ground ! Freed from the great strain and waste
which all this system creates, the body politic
will recover like a man from a disease, and spring
to unexpected powers of health.

Meanwhile in the great industrial associations,
voluntary and other, folk will have been learning
the sentiment of the Common Life—the habit of
acting together for common ends, the habit of
feeling together for common interests—and once

---

[1] This alleviation indeed is already in some curious ways
visible. Forty years ago the few dressed in broadcloth,
the masses in fustian ; but now that silk is made out of wood-
pulp, and everybody can dress and does dress in the latest
fashion, it is no distinction to have fine clothes. Similarly
with books, travel, and a hundred other things. What is
the good of being a millionaire when the man with three
pounds a week can make almost as good a show as you ?

this has been learnt, the rest will follow of its own accord.

In the course of these changes, moving always towards a non - governmental and perfectly voluntary society in the end, it is probable that some Property-founded institutions, like the payment of labor by wages, though not exactly ideal in their character, will continue for a long period. It may perhaps be said that in some ways a generous wage-payment convention (as for instance sketched in the last chapter of Carruthers' *Commercial and Communal Economy*) on a thoroughly democratic basis, gives more freedom than a formless Anarchism in which each one takes " according to his needs," simply because under the first system *A* could work two hours a day and live on the wage of two, and *B* could work eight and live on the wage of eight, each with perfect moral freedom—whereas if there was no wage system, *A* (however much he might wish to loaf) would feel that he was cheating the community—and the community would think so too—unless he gave his eight hours like everybody else.[1]

The great point however to bear in mind in all this matter is that though the Cash nexus may and no doubt will linger on for a long time

[1] It is difficult also to see how things like railways and the immense modern industries (if these survive) could be carried on without some such system of wage-payment and the definite engagement to fulfil certain work which it carries with it.

in various forms of Wages, Purchase, Sale, and so forth, it must inevitably with the changing sentiment and conditions of life lose its cast-iron stringent character, and gradually be converted into the elastic cord, which while it may indicate a line of social custom will yield to pressure when the need arises. Private Property will thus lose its present virulent character, and subside into a matter of mere use or convenience ; monetary reckonings and transfers, as time goes on, will seem little more than formalities—as to-day between friends.

Finally, Custom alone will remain. The subsidence of the Property feeling will mean the subsidence of brute-force Law, for whose existence Property is mainly responsible. The peoples accustomed to the varied activities of a complex industrial organism, will still—though not suffering from the compulsion either of hunger or of brute authority—continue through custom to carry on those activities, their Reason in the main approving.

Custom will remain—slowly changing. And the form of the Societies of the future will be more vital and organic, and far more truly human, than they have been or could be under the rigid domination of Law.

VI

SMALL HOLDINGS AND AGRICULTURAL
CO-OPERATION

IN my experience Small Holders are among the
best and most capable of our rural populations.
I include as small holders those who work farms
up to forty acres or so.[1] They generally exhibit
a good deal of all-round capacity, and are
versatile and handy at a variety of jobs. And
this for the simple reason that having to look
after a small place mainly by themselves they
are *obliged* to be a little ingenious and versatile.
Such a man, besides the farmwork connected with
the animals and the crops, generally knows something of joinering and iron work ; he has a bench
and a few tools, and an old anvil picked up at
a sale ; he personally repairs his sheds and outhouses, or (if he is a freeholder) builds new
ones ; he does a little thatching ; and in many
cases—especially if his holding is really small—
he is compelled to earn something by outside
work for neighbors, by doing a bit of gardening,
or masoning or walling from time to time. Thus

[1] The Small Holdings Act of 1907 includes anything from
one acre up to fifty acres.

such a man is often very resourceful, and in a sense well-educated, even though he may only read or write with difficulty.

On a large farm there is almost too much division of labor. There are several farm-hands, and one is cowman and another plowman and a third horseman, and so on ; and I find they tend consequently to drop into grooves and become rather limited in their outlook and acti-vities. The farmer, instead of *compelling* a change of occupation now and then, takes the easiest line and allows the young men—even though they be his own sons—to remain in their grooves, and consequently to grow up somewhat stunted in ability and ignorant of a large portion of their proper business.

For this reason alone—namely, the production of handy capable men (and women)—Small Holdings are much to be encouraged. If the men and women of a country are (as they cer-tainly are) its most important crop, this is a matter which demands attention. The decay of the townbred peoples—the puny sickly character of the crowds that are the product of the factories and offices of our big towns—is a menace to our civilisation ; and if at the same time the present depopulation of the country-sides is going to continue the situation will become very serious. We want to get a far larger population on the land, and so to produce a far larger amount of home-grown food than we do at present. Pro-

ductive self-support has in fact become imperative. It has been calculated that if the United
Kingdom were only cultivated to the same degree
that Belgium was before the Great War it would
supply home-grown food for 37 million people
instead of for 17 million as now ; and there
is no doubt that an equal or even greater degree
of cultivation is quite possible here—with due
organisation and intelligence. We have heard
a good deal lately about our dependence on the
imports of food from abroad. In 1905 the
imports of butter, cheese, milk (condensed),
bacon, lard, fowls, eggs, onions and potatoes,
amounted to £58,000,000 in value—the value in
eggs alone being nearly £7,000,000. All these
articles, and many others, including apples, pears,
small fruits, honey, and many vegetables, are
particularly suited for being grown on small
holdings, but (partly owing to the dearth of
such holdings) have been much neglected, and
their place taken by foreign produce. The importance of getting the additional population on
the land which an extension of small cultivation
would mean, and at the same time of securing so
great an augmentation of our food supply, can
hardly be overestimated. It ought to be one
of the very first things to be considered in the
reorganisation of our industrial system.[1]

[1] "In France, before the loss of Alsace-Lorraine there
were about five *million* proprietors owning seven and a half
acres each on the average ; and in Würtemburg 260,000

It must not be forgotten too that an increased (productive) country population would supply an extra market for our townmade manufactured goods, and so again be helpful in making the whole community self-contained and independent of foreign influences. Not that foreign trade is in itself a thing undesirable ; but it always has to be remembered that to be dependent on influences which we cannot control is a mistake ; also that, other things being equal, to exchange goods at home is better than to exchange the same abroad, simply because the cost of shipping or carriage is so much less in the former instance.

There are other things to be said in favor of small holdings. One is that they constitute a ' ladder ' by which the agricultural laborer or even the townsman may climb up to a substantial position on the land. The younger son of a farmer, for instance, does not generally see any prospect of coming into the farm himself. He cannot command enough capital to take another large farm and stock it, and if he cannot find a small holding suited to his means there is nothing left for him but to become a farm servant or to migrate into town life. Naturally he adopts the latter alternative. It is often said that the depopulation of the country-sides is due to the inordinate desire of country lads for

peasant owners with less than five acres each, and 160,000 with over five acres each " (pamphlet by J. B. Paton on the *Peasantry of England*, Manchester, 1901).

the excitements of city life. I do not find it so. More often they are simply driven into the towns by the necessity of earning a living somewhere, and by the closure of all avenues of decent life in the country. It goes without saying that long hours, wretched wages, and the dulness of life under the regime of the squire and the parson, contribute to this result. If we are to have an intelligent and alert population on the land (a *sine qua non* of any nation's greatness) the land must be made attractive and accessible, and one means towards this is the encouragement of small holdings.

Hitherto we may almost say any development in this direction had been *dis*couraged in this country by those who have most sway in the matter—the landlord class. There are several reasons for this. One undoubtedly is that small holders as a rule—whether freeholders or tenants —are not ' respectable ' enough to suit the gentry. They are too democratic. People who have a little independence of habit and manner, who do not salute their superiors becomingly, or who build with their own hands ramshackle sheds and outhouses in their fields, are obviously not to be encouraged. And what is more serious, such people are a great bar to ' sport.' Foxes are liable to be trapped or poisoned by them. To hunt or shoot over their little holdings is to run the risk of having a wasp's nest stirred about one's ears and to court all sorts of unpleasantnesses. For indeed a landowner who has five or six large farmers for his tenants can fairly easily come to terms with these in the matter of hunting and shooting, but what could he do with fifty or a hundred small holders? The thing would be impossible.[1]

It is somewhat the same with regard to Rents. The landlord or his agent finds it much easier and simpler to collect rents from a few large holders than from a great many small ones. Hence there is a tendency for convenience' sake towards large holdings. In the middle and later part of last century the rolling up of small farms into large ones went on apace. To-day there is beginning to be a tendency the other way ; but the breaking up process and the providing of barns and cottages for the subdivided portions is a laborious and expensive matter, and at present is only moving slowly. Of course this matter of the size of farms is also largely a question of the kind of crops arranged for or desired. Where cereals or root crops are wanted large holdings and agricultural machines of various kinds are much to the point, but the equally valuable and often more valuable supplies of vegetables, small fruit, orchard fruit, eggs, etc., are best grown on small places where individual attention is the main thing and machinery is less important.

One common objection brought against the

[1] See Ch. VII, *infra.*

small holding idea is that little industries work at a disadvantage in point of capital, division of labor, sheer productiveness, etc., as compared with large-scale industries. Of course there is a certain amount of truth in this—though it would not do to say that *all* small-scale industries suffer in the comparison—and if it were the case that the absolute and only object of industry was the money-value of its product there would be still more truth in it ; but we have seen through that delusion already, and need not again be led astray by it.

The limitation, however, of his Capital, in the case of a small man, his disadvantage in the markets, both in buying and selling, his being compelled sometimes to invest in a horse and cart or in some kind of machinery which the exiguity of his estate will not permit him fully to use, the difficulty that he has in borrowing money in a time of need, and the danger of falling into the hands of the money-lender—all these things undoubtedly do militate against the small holder ; and the cure for them equally undoubtedly is to be found in Co-operation.

The classical instance of the value of Co-operation in connexion with small holdings is to be found in Denmark. After 1864, when Germany had wrested Schleswig-Holstein from the Danes, there was nothing left for the latter but to make the best of what remained to them.

Jutland was little better than a sandy heath ; but
with extraordinary energy the people threw themselves into its development ; the soil was worked
and enriched in every possible way ; the land
was broken up into holdings of seven to ten
acres each ; sheds and cots and cottages were
erected ; co-operative societies were formed
among the settlers ; the government helped with
agricultural organisation, the creation of High
Schools for the peasants, and the loan of funds ;
and before long there were beside large farms
some 150,000 little holdings of seven to ten acres
successfully running there, whose activities were
largely carried on by combined labor. The
first co-operative dairy was started in 1882 ; by
the year 1904 there were over 1,000 such dairies.
Bacon-curing, the collecting and sale of eggs,
poultry, honey, the manufacture of butter and
cheese, the purchase of seeds, food-stuffs,
manures, machinery, were all negotiated by the
same method ; insurance and banking the same ;
and in this short period of time sandy Jutland
became a large exporter of food, and poured
even into England (with its really richer soil)
great quantities of farm-produce which England
might have been growing for herself. In the
form of butter, eggs and bacon alone Denmark
before the War was supplying the United Kingdom to the value of 15 or 20 million sterling.[1]

[1] See also article on "Co-operation in Denmark," by Erik
Givskov in the *Wholesale Co-operative Annual* for 1905.

France, Belgium, Holland, Norway, Sweden, Finland, Italy, Roumania, Bulgaria, have followed on the same lines of agricultural co-operation. Nor must we forget Ireland. The noble efforts of Horace Plunkett and afterwards of George Russell (A.E.) were scoffed at at first. But gradually they won their way. In 1889, I believe, the first Irish Creamery was started ; in 1895 there were already 67 ; and in 1902, over 320, effecting sales to the value of £1,000,000 per annum ; to-day there are agricultural societies without end, for the production and sale of poultry, eggs, flax, fruit, honey, and a variety of other things.

Mr. George Russell, in his excellent book *The National Being*,[1] shows from his own experience what the co-operative association can do. He says (p. 46) : " The Society is a better buyer than the individual. It can buy things the individual cannot buy. It is a better producer also. The plant for a creamery is beyond the individual farmer ; but our organised farmers in Ireland, small though they are, find it no trouble to erect and equip a creamery with plant costing £2,000. The organised rural community of the future will generate its own electricity at its central buildings, and run not only its factories and other enterprises by this power, but will supply light to the houses of its members and also mechanical power to run machinery on the

Maunsel & Co., Dublin and London, 1916, price 4s. 6d.

farm. One of our Irish societies already supplies electric light for the town it works in. In the organised rural community the eggs, milk, poultry, pigs, cattle, grain and wheat produced on the farm and not consumed or required for further agricultural production, will automatically be delivered to the co-operative business centre of the district, where the manager of the dairy will turn the milk into butter or cheese, and the skim milk will be returned to feed the community's pigs. The poultry and egg department will pack and dispatch the fowls and eggs to market. The mill will grind the corn, and return it ground to the member, or there may be a co-operative bakery to which some of it may go." And so on. A picture follows of how the rural labourers under this regime will gradually become skilled co-workers with one another, and the co-operative community have its own carpenters, smiths and mechanics ; how there will be common laundries and kitchens, and village halls with libraries and gymnasiums and rooms for recreation and dancing. All very feasible, and one may say already realised in part in various different localities.

The matter of co-operative banks is important. At present a small man who wants £20 to pay his rent with is very much put to it if he does not happen to have that amount in hand—even though he knows that in a couple of months he will be quite well off. If he goes to the ordinary Bank to borrow he is treated with scant respect and made to understand that owing to deficient security he will have to pay a high rate of interest. The alternative for the wretched man is to sell a cow, which he often has to do, owing to the forced sale, at a decided loss. [And there are, I need hardly say, some speculative dealers who count on this sort of thing and make a *practice* of purchasing from small men in distress. The co-operative Bank is a quite different affair. The farmers of a certain district club together for financial purposes. Having between them all a great amount of valuable farm stock, machinery, etc., it becomes possible for the Club to go to an ordinary commercial Bank and borrow on this joint security. The security in the mass being thoroughly good the Bank will probably, as things are, lend at 4 per cent. interest. The Club will borrow just as much as it needs, and lend the money out, if required, to its members—of course at a rather higher rate of interest, say 5 per cent. The extra 1 per cent. so coming in will pay the secretarial and other expenses of the Club. Now the Club, or its committee, knowing well the financial circumstances of its members, will have no difficulty in deciding in each case on what conditions, of interest or repayment, the loan shall be afforded. It will only perhaps be very rarely that interest exceeding 5 per cent. will be demanded. Suppose a small man wishes to borrow, as above,

a sum of £20 to pay his rent. He only wants
the loan for a couple of months, as he will be
able to repay it before then, and he gets the
money from his Club at 5 per cent. Five per
cent. on £20 for a year would be £1 ; but for
those two months it will only amount to 3s. 4d. ;
and he obtains this great accommodation for that
trifling sum. This is a good deal better than
having to sell his cow at a breakneck price.

In many cases the combination of a large farm
with a number of small holdings and village
industries in a kind of co-operative Colony may
prove very desirable, and it is much to be hoped
that this form of settlement on the land may
be carried out in the future. Let us suppose
that 2,000 acres of good farm land are purchased and properly equipped with buildings and
machinery and live stock, and that out of this
or in connexion with it sufficient land is set apart
for twenty or thirty small holdings, with suitable
cottages and barns. Then a good farm-manager
working the central farm would have beside his
regular staff a supply of men from the small
holdings to do wage-work when necessary on the
farm. On the other hand as a skilled agriculturist he would be able to advise the small
holders about their crops and their animals ; he
would organise for them co-operative purchase
of food-stuffs, etc., or co-operative sale of their
produce. Moreover a number of the small men
would probably have command of useful trades,

such as blacksmithing, building, joinering, tailor-
ing and so forth ; and so a competent head
man might in this way build up a largely self-
contained and at any rate self-supporting Colony
—in which all the members would take some
share in the work, and of course derive a corresponding share of the profits.

Colony or no Colony, the combination of a
small holding with some technical or industrial
occupation is a great help. There are always
times when work on the land is not needed, or
if needed not feasible, and in such times a small
trade is a great financial resource. In this way
smithing, as I have said, or joinering or cabinet-
making, or masoning, or boot or sandal making,
or bookbinding, engraving, literary and art work,
teaching, commercial traveling, and many other
activities may be worked in with the agricultural
life, and with really great advantage to both sides.

In the matter of the purchase or acquirement
by individuals of such holdings—either freehold
or on a long lease—Co-operation naturally comes
in again. In the neighborhood where I am
living—while fields adjacent to the roads and
eligible for building command something like
£100 per acre—large farms of 50 or 100 acres
can often be bought in bulk for £25 per acre.
Needless to say that it is good business for a
group co-operatively to purchase such a farm
and subdivide it themselves according to their
needs—the low price enabling them jointly to

make accommodation roads, erect fences, etc. ; and such a group may naturally combine for further purposes, like buying and selling, when once the holdings are fairly established and in operation. When the Land Valuation Acts are once supplemented by a " Tax and Buy " ordinance, allowing public bodies to purchase lands on a fair basis of their estimated rental for rating purposes, some millions of acres now held up in private ownership for sporting or other non-productive uses will come into the market, and be available for the objects indicated in this chapter. I have on more than one occasion had reason to mention the case of some moors near here which till lately carried for rating purposes an estimated rental of only 2s. 6d. per acre, and which yet were charged to a public body for reservoir needs at the rate of over £100 per acre ! [1]

In England the Small Holdings and Agricultural Co-operation movement progresses only slowly—though a few large owners like Lord Carrington and Mr. Winfrey in Norfolk and Lincolnshire, and Sir Robert Edgcumbe in Dorset, and a few societies like the A.O.S., have done their best for it. But the Government and the official people have been very slack and have not seemed to realise the importance of the matter ; while the farmers have commonly been rather hostile than otherwise. Thus it has come

[1] See Ch. VII, *infra.*

about that while Ireland in such things is on the forefront of the wave of progress England is still waterlogged (water on the brain !) and in the trough of the sea.

The English mind, being relatively incapable of reasoning, only moves as a rule under the stimulus of felt necessity or of a visible object-lesson. Start a Creamery or Co-operative Dairy in a certain locality, and the people of the neighborhood will come to see, and will possibly in the end follow the example in their own villages, but you may *talk* and *lecture* to them without end and still without result. An amusing illustration of this concrete habit of the English mind occurred at Brandsby in Yorkshire at the beginning of the County Council's agricultural lectures in that region. An expert came there weekly to give lectures on Dairy Work and butter making. The attendance at the first lecture was poor and disappointing. At its conclusion a farm-man got up and said that *he* didn't see the good of a " gentleman " coming down to lecture to them on dairy work " what had probably never milked a cow in his life." Luckily the lecturer knew his business and immediately replied, " Well, I'll milk a cow against *you* any day." Great excitement ! The challenge was accepted, and it was agreed that at the next week's meeting there should be two cows on the platform, and the competitors should toss up for their choice. The news spread through the

8

village, and whereas the lecture-room at the first meeting had been almost empty, at the second it was full to overflowing. The lecturer fortunately won easily, getting more milk from his cow, and in less time, than the other ; and after that, needless to say, the course was a great success.

This concrete habit and tendency to rely only on actual experience has, of course, its good side ; and our County Councils and other authorities, taking up the cue, should do their best to dot the country-sides with effective examples of small holdings co-operatively organised.

VII

THE VILLAGE AND THE LANDLORD [1]

MY object in this paper is simply to describe
the economic conditions of a single country parish,
here in England, and from the consideration of
these conditions to draw some inferences towards
our future policy with regard to the land. In
modern life—in every department of it, one may
say—bedrock facts are so veiled over by complex
and adventitious growths that it is difficult to
see the proper and original outline of any problem
with which we are dealing ; and so it certainly
is in this matter of the land question. Any one
glancing at a country village, say in the neighborhood of London, probably sees a mass of
villas, people hurrying to a railway station, motor-
cars, and so forth ; but as to where the agricultural workers are, what they are doing, how they
live, what their relations may be to the land and
the land owners—these things are obscure, not
easily seen, and difficult to get information about.
And yet these are the things, one may say, which
are most vital, most important.

[1] Published also (in 1909) as a Fabian Tract, No. 136.

The parish which I have in mind to describe is a rather large and straggling parish in a rural district, with a small population, some 500 souls, almost entirely agricultural in character, consisting of farmers, farm laborers, woodmen, and so forth, with a few miners and small artisans—on the whole a pretty hard-working, industrious lot. Fortunately, one may say, there is hardly anything resembling a villa in the whole parish ; there is no resident squire, and the business man is conspicuous by his absence. The place therefore forms a good example for the study of the agricultural land question. The farms are not over large, being mostly between fifty and one hundred acres in extent. There is just the land, and the population living mainly by the cultivation of it. This population, as I have hinted, is not lacking in industry ; it is fairly healthy and well grown ; there is no severe poverty ; and (probably owing to the absence of the parasite classes) it is better off than most of our agricultural populations. Yet it is poor, one may almost say very poor. Probably, of the hundred families in the parish, the *average* income is not much over £60 a year ; and many, of course, can by no means reach even that standard.

Let us consider some of the financial and other conditions which lead to this state of affairs. In the first place, I find that the inhabitants have to pay in actual rent to their landlords about

£2,500 a year. In fact, the gross estimated rental of the parish is about £3,250, but as there are quite a few small freeholders the amount actually paid in rent is reduced to £2,500. Nearly the whole of this goes off out of the parish and never comes back again. The duke and most of the other landlords are absentees. This forms at once, as is obvious, a severe tax on the inhabitants. One way or another the hundred families out of what they produce from the land have to pay £2,500 a year into alien hands— or, averaging it, £25 per family! and this, if their average income is now only £60, is certainly a heavy burden; since, if they had not to pay this sum, their income might be £85. No doubt it will be said, "Here we see the advantage of having resident squires. The money would then return to the parish." But would it? Would it return to those who produced it? No; it would not. The spoliation of the toilers would only be disguised, not remedied. In fact, let us suppose (a quite ordinary case) that the parish in question were owned by a single resident squire, and that the £2,500 were paid to him in rent. That rent would only go to support a small extra population of servants and dependents in the place. One or two small shops might be opened; but to the farmer and farm worker no advantage would accrue. There might be a slightly increased sale of milk and eggs; but this again would be countervailed by many disadvantages. " Sport " over all the farm lands would become a chronic nuisance ; the standard and cost of living, dress, etc., would be raised ; and the feeble and idiotic life of the " gentry," combined with their efforts to patronise and intimidate, would go far to corrupt the population generally. In this parish then, of which I am speaking, the people may be truly thankful that they have not any resident squires. All the same, the tax of £25 per family is levied upon them to support such squires in some place or other, and is a permanent burden upon their lives.

Less than a hundred years ago there were in this parish extensive common lands. In fact, of the 4,600 acres of which the parish consists, 2,650, or considerably more than half, were commons. They were chiefly moors and woods ; but were, needless to say, very valuable to cottagers and small farmers. Here was pasture for horses, cows, sheep, pigs, geese ; here in the woods was firewood to be got, and bracken for bedding ; on the moors, rabbits, bilberries, turf for fuel, etc. In 1820 these commons were enclosed ; and this is another thing that has helped to cripple the lives of the inhabitants. As is well known, during all that period systematic enclosure of the common lands of Great Britain was going on. In a landlord House of Parliament it was easy enough to get bills passed. Any stick will do to beat a dog with ; and it was easy to say that these lands, being common lands, were not so well cultivated as they might be, and that *therefore* the existing landlords ought to share them up. The logic might not be very convincing, but it served its purpose. The landlords appropriated the common lands ; and during the 120 years from 1760 to 1880, *ten millions of acres* in Great Britain were thus enclosed.[1]

In 1820 the turn of this particular parish came, and its 2,650 acres of commons " went in." I used to know an old man of the locality who remembered when they " went in." He used to speak of the occurrence as one might speak of a sinister and fatal event of nature—a landslide or an earthquake. There was no idea that it could have been prevented. The commons simply went in ! The country folk witnessed the proceeding with dismay ; but, terrorised by their landlords, and with no voice in Parliament, they were helpless.

It may be interesting to see some of the details of the operation. In the Enclosure Award Book, still kept in the parish, there remains a full account. The then Duke of Rutland, as lord of the manor, as impropriator for tithes, as proprietor, and so forth, got the lion's share, nearly 2,000 acres. The remaining 650 acres went to the other landlords. Certain manorial and tithe rights were remitted as a kind of compensation,

[1] See Mulhall's *Dictionary of Statistics*, " Enclosures."

and the thing was done.   In the Award Book
the duke's share is given as follows :—

		Acres.	Roods.
1.	"As Impropriator for tithes of corn, grain, and hay ; and in lieu of and full compensation for all manner of tithes, both great and small"	1,381	3
2.	"As Lord of the Manor," and in compensation for certain manorial rights, " and for his consent to the said enclosure " ...	108	2
3.	" For chief rents," amounting in the whole to £14	28	2
4.	"For enfranchisement of copyholds"	11	3
5.	"As proprietor "	18	2
6.	"By sale to defray the expenses of the Act"	449	1
		1,998	1

Thus we find, in exchange for the ducal tithes,
nearly a third of the whole area of the parish
handed over—most of it certainly not the best
lands, but lands having considerable value as
woods and moors.   We find some acres adjudged
to the duke in consideration of his kind " consent " to the transaction.   And, most wonderful
of all, nearly 450 acres surrendered by the parish
to defray the expenses of getting the Act through
Parliament !   And now to-day in the said parish
there is not a little field or corner left—absolutely
not a solitary acre out of all the vast domain
which was once for the people's use—on which
the village boys can play their game of cricket !

Indeed, most valuable tracts were enclosed quite in the centre of the village itself—as, for instance, a piece which is still called " The Common," though it is no longer common, and many bits on which little cottages had been erected by quite small folk. It would be a very desirable thing that the enclosure award books in other parishes should be investigated, and the corresponding facts with regard to the ancient commons brought to light generally over the country.[1]

A third thing which cripples the agricultural interest very considerably is the incidence of the rates. The farmer's dread of a rise in rates has become almost proverbial. And it is by no means unnatural or unreasonable. For there is probably no class whose estimated rental is so large, compared with their actual net income, as the farmer class. A farmer whose farm, after deducting all expenses of rent, rates, manure, wages, etc., yields him a clear profit of no more than £100 a year for his household use is quite probably paying £70 a year in rent. But a superior artisan or small professional man who is making £150 a year will very likely be only paying £20 in rent. It is obvious that any slight increase in the rates will fall much more heavily on the first man than on the second. The rates, therefore, are a serious matter to the farmer ;

[1] *Some Forgotten Facts in the History of Sheffield and District* (Independent Press, Sheffield, 1907, price 2s. 6d.) contains valuable information of this kind.

and something in the way of shifting their incidence, and distributing the burden more fairly,
ought certainly to be done.[1]

As an instance of this latter point, let me
again refer to the parish in question. We have
seen that some 2,600 acres of common lands
passed over to the landlords in 1820, ostensibly
for the public advantage and benefit. Of these,
more than 1,500 acres of moor land, held by the
duke, are rated on an estimated rental of less
than 2s. 6d. per acre. The general farm lands
of the parish are rated on an estimated rental of
14s. or 15s. per acre on the average. Thus the
moor lands are assessed at about one-sixth of
the value of the farm lands. This is perhaps
excessively low ; but the matter might pass, if
it were not for a somewhat strange fact—namely
that a few years ago when some twenty acres
of these very moor lands were wanted for a matter
of great public advantage and benefit, that is,
for the formation of a reservoir, the ducal estate
could not part with them under £50 an acre ;
and a little later, when an extension of acreage
was required, the district council had to pay a
much higher price, so that the total purchase,
first and last, comes out at more than £150 per

[1] I am not here discussing the question of how far a rise
of rates falls upon the landlord ; for, though this may ultimately and in the far distance be so, it is clear that the
farmer primarily feels the pinch, and not till he is nearly
ruined is there any chance of his getting a corresponding
abatement of rent.

acre ! Now here is something very seriously out of joint. Either the moor lands are worth a capital value of £150 an acre, in which case they ought to be assessed at, say £5, instead of at 2s. 6d. ; or else, if the rating at 2s. 6d. is really just and fair, surely it is monstrous that the public, having to carry through a most important and necessary improvement, should be " held up " and made to pay a ruinous price, simply because the land cannot be obtained elsewhere. The conclusion is : Let such lands be rated in accordance with the capital value set upon them by their owners, and we shall have a much fairer and more equitable distribution of the public burden.

And this matter of the moors leads to the consideration of a fourth cause which cripples the land cultivator terribly in this country. I mean Sport. The nuisance and detriment that this is to the farmer has become so great that, unless strict measures are soon taken, widespread ruin will ensue. In many subtle ways this acts. With the enormous growth of wealthy and luxurious classes during the last fifty years, the tendency has been to turn the country districts into a mere playground. The very meaning of the word sport has changed. The careful working of covers by the occasional sportsman has been replaced by clumsy battues, with wild shouts and shrieks of " drivers," and huge slaughter of birds, half tame, and specially bred for the purpose.

Mobs of people, anxious to appear fashionable, and rigged out by their tailors in befitting costume, are formed into shooting parties. Rich men, wanting to get into society, hire moors and woods, regardless of expense, regardless of animal slaughter, regardless of agricultural interests, as long as they get an opportunity to invite their friends.[1] In Devonshire to-day the farms in many parts are simply eaten up by rabbits, because the landlords, in order to provide plenty of shooting, insist on spinneys and copses and hedgerows and waste bits being retained in their wild state for purposes of cover! On the northern moors the rabbits simply devastate the farms along the moor edges—not because the rabbits are preserved, for the shooting is mainly of grouse and pheasants, but because the moors, being uncared for except in this way, the rabbits are allowed to multiply without check. They are the gamekeeper's perquisite. Yet if the farmer who has a farm adjoining the moor carries a gun to protect himself against their invasions, it is conveyed to him (if a

[1] The financing of these affairs is funny. A large moor will let for the grouse season for £3,000, say on the condition of grouse being bagged up to, but not beyond, 2,400 brace. Mid-week parties hurry in by rail and motor, stay for two or, perhaps, three nights, and hurry off again, to be succeeded by other parties the following weeks. The whole thing is conducted in the most mechanical way, with "drives," "batteries," and so forth. And when the expenses are added up, including men employed, guests entertained, and rent paid, they certainly do not fall far short of the proverbial guinea a bird!

tenant of the same landlord) that he had better not do so, lest he should be suspected of shooting the grouse ! Thus he is paralysed from his own defence. In the parish of which I am speaking there are lands along the moor edges which used to grow oats and other crops, but which now, on account of the rabbit nuisance, are quite un-cultivable in that way, and only yield the barest pasture.

In and about 1850, when wheat more than once reached £5 a quarter, the farmers and landlords were doing a roaring trade. Rents were high, but the land could afford it. Farmers were anxious to increase the size of their holdings, and landlords were not averse to this, as it saved them trouble. And so set in that tendency to roll small holdings into big ones which continued, with baneful effect, during all the second half of the century. Sport at the same time came in to increase the action. It was easier to pacify the few than the many over the matter. It was simpler to hunt a pack of hounds over two or three large farms than across a network of small holdings. Besides, the New Rich, as well as the elder gentry, wanted widespread parks, and not a democratic rabble of cottagers at their very doors. And so the game went on. Soon prices of farmstuff fell heavily. But it is easier to get rents up than to get them down again. The alleviations of rent which *have* taken place since 1854 have been only painfully gained and grudgingly yielded. Wheat which was at 100 shillings a quarter then fetched only about 30 shillings at the beginning of this century ! And though other farmstuffs have not fallen in like degree, yet during all that period of declining prices, the British farmer has been pinched and pined all over the country. The landlord has been on top of him ; and with holdings often much too large for his need, and a yearly balance too small, he has employed far less labor and tillage than he ought to have done ; his land has lost heart ; and he has lost heart—till he has become to-day probably the least enterprising and least up to date of all the agriculturists of Western Europe.[1]

Such are some at least of the causes which have contributed to the decay of agriculture in this country ; and their consideration may indicate the directions in which to seek for a cure.

What is needed, first and foremost, is very obviously security of tenure, under such conditions as shall give both farmer and cottager a powerful interest in the land and its improvement. It is often said, and supposed, that the countryman nowadays does not care about the land and the rural life, and is longing to exchange it for town life. I do not find this so. I find that he is compelled into town life by the hard conditions

[1] There are many farms of 500 or 600 acres in Gloucestershire only employing five or six hands—or one man to a hundred acres !

which prevail in the country—but not that he *wants* to leave the latter. Indeed, I am amazed at the tenacity with which he clings to the land, despite the long hours and the heavy toil ; nor can one witness without wonder and admiration the really genuine interest which he feels in its proper treatment, quite apart from any advantage or disadvantage to himself. It is common to find a farm laborer expressing satisfaction or disgust at the good or bad tillage of a field with which he is in no way connected ; or to see a small farmer's son working early and late, perhaps up to the age of thirty, with no wages but a mere pittance in the way of pocket-money, and only a remote prospect of inheriting at some future date his share of the farm-stock and savings, and yet taking a wholehearted interest in the work not really different from that which an artist may feel. There is some splendid material here —in these classes neglected by the nation, and overlaid by a tawdry and cheap-jack civilisation.

I say it is clear that they must be given a secure and liberal tenure of the land and be free once for all from the caprice of the private land-lord with his insolences of political intimidation and sport, and his overbearance in parochial affairs. The absolute speechlessness of our rural workers to-day on all matters of public interest is clearly, to any one who knows them, due to their mortal dread lest their words should reach the powers above. It has become an ingrained habit. And it has led of course to a real paralysis of their thinking capacity and their enterprise. But place these men in a position where the fruits of their toil will be secure, where improvements can be made, in cottage or farm, with a sense of ownership, and where their vote and voice in the councils of the parish will not be dependent on squire or parson ; and the world will be astonished at the result.

There are two main directions in which to go in the matter of secure tenure. One is the creation of more small freeholds ; the other is the throwing of lands into the hands of public authorities, and the creation of permanent tenures under them. Though the latter embodies the best general principle, I do not think that forms a reason for ruling out freeholds *altogether*. In all these matters variety is better than uniformity ; and a certain number of freeholds would probably be desirable. In the same way with regard to public ownership, if anything like nationalisation of the land is effected, I think it should decidedly be on the same principle of variety—creating not only State and municipal ownership, but ownership by county councils, district councils, parish councils, etc.—with a leaning perhaps towards the more *local* authorities, because the needs of particular lands and the folk occupying them are likely on the whole to be better understood and allowed for in the locality than from a distance.

Let us suppose, in the parish which I have

taken for my text, that by some kind of political miracle, all the lands on which rents are now being paid to absent landlords were transferred to the ownership of the Parish Council. Then at once the latter body would come into an income of £2,500 a year. At one blow the whole burden of the rates would fall off, and still a large balance be left for public works and improvements of all kinds. It might be allowable, for a moment, to draw a picture of the utopian conditions which would ensue—the rates all paid, the rents milder and more equal than before, the wages of parish workers raised, free meals for school-children provided, capital available for public buildings, free libraries, agricultural engines and machinery, also for improving or administering common lands and woods, and so forth. There is no danger of course of so delirious an embarrassment occurring! for any scheme of nationalisation would take a long time, and would only gradually culminate ; and no scheme would place the whole lands of a parish at the disposal of a single body like the parish council. But the example helps us to realise the situation. Every farmer and cottager whose holding was under a public body would know and feel that whatever rent he might have to pay, it would come back to him in public advantages, in the ordaining of which he would have a voice ; he would know that he would be in no danger of disturbance as long as he paid his rent ; and

9

in the matter of capital improvements in land or building he might either make them himself (with the council's consent), in which case if he should decide later on to quit the holding, the council would compensate him, knowing that the rental paid by the new tenant would be correspondingly increased ; or he could get the council (if willing) to make the improvement, and himself pay a correspondingly increased rent for it. In either case he would have as good a bargain, and almost as free a hand, as if he were on his own freehold.

Security of tenure, largely through public ownership, must certainly be one of the first items of a land-reform program. Another item, the importance of which is now being widely felt, is the making provision for the effective supply of small holdings. The Small Holdings and Allotments Act (of 1907) has not so far borne much fruit. Indeed, one rather gathers that forces purposely hostile to it have been at work. But this state of affairs must not continue ; and some advance in that direction will certainly have to be effected. By small holdings I mean holdings, freehold or leasehold, from twenty-five acres down to one or two acres in extent, each with cottage and buildings attached. Of holdings of this class (largely owing to the " rolling up " policy of last century) there is an absolute famine in the land. The demand, the outcry, for them is great, but the supply is most scanty. Yet this class covers some of the most important work of modern agriculture, and a great variety of such work. It includes, in its smaller sizes, market gardens, with intensive culture of all kinds, and glass, besides the kind of holding occupied by the professional man or other worker who supplements his income by some small cultivation ; and in its larger sizes it includes nurseries, as well as small arable and pasture farms. The starvation that exists to-day in Britain of all these classes of industry is a serious matter.[1]

In the parish with which we are dealing, owing partly to its distance from a market, the demand for such holdings takes chiefly the form of a demand for small arable and pasture farms. But the need of these is great, as indeed it is nearly all over the country. A holding of this kind, of any size from five to twenty acres, forms an excellent stepping-stone, as I have said (p. 102), for a farm laborer or farmer's son towards a position of independence. A second or third son of a farmer, not likely to follow his father in the occupation of the

[1] It will be said that if there is such a demand for small holdings, the supply will soon by natural laws be forthcoming. But as a matter of fact under our present system this is not so—and for three reasons: (1) the slowness of the landed classes to perceive the needs of the day—even though to their own interest ; (2) the want of capital among a great number of them, which makes them unwilling to face the breaking up of large farms and the building of extra cottages ; (3) the fact that those who have money are careless about public needs, and do not *want* to see a sturdy population of small holders about their doors.

farm, has to-day only a poor prospect. Unable to command enough capital to stock a large farm himself, and unable to find a small one, he has but two alternatives—to drift down into the fruit-less life of the farm laborer, or else to go off and try his luck in town. If, as is most often the case, he is twenty-five or so before the need of making a decision comes upon him, his chances of learning a town trade are closed, and the first alternative is all that is left. Yet the small holder of this kind is often one of the most effective and useful types of agricultural worker. On a holding, say of fifteen acres, while he cannot get an adequate living for himself and family by ordinary farm methods, yet he can gain a considerable amount, which he supplements by working as a useful hand for neighbors at harvest and other times. Being thrown on his resources, and not having *too* much land, he gains more than the average out of it, and his own ingenuities and capacities are developed ; so that, as a rule, he is the most resourceful and capable type of man in the district. It is of the most vital importance to the country that this type of man, and his class of holding, should be encouraged.

There is one method which I have so far neglected to mention by which both security of tenure and small holdings can be obtained—I mean Co-operation. The formation of co-opera-tive societies for the purchase of large farms, for the division of them, the building of cottages,

and the leasing of small holdings so obtained, is
one of the most hopeful directions for the future.
It ought to be easy for the public authorities to
lend money on perfectly safe terms for this
purpose. What co-operation has done and is
doing for agriculture in other countries—in the
way of establishing banks, land-holding societies,
societies for butter-making, egg-collecting, buying
of feeding stuffs and manures, sale of produce,
etc., is now perfectly well known. Ireland even
has left England behind in this matter ; but
England and Scotland will have to level up. It
is a sign, at least of good intentions, that the
late Act gives power to the County Councils to
promote and assist the formation and working
of co - operative agricultural societies of all
kinds.

One of the very first things, I think, which
ought to be taken up is this question of the
commons. If ten million acres between 1760
and 1880 passed so easily from the public use
into the exclusive hands of the landowners, surely
there ought not to be much difficulty in passing
them back again. As I have said, they were
appropriated mainly on the plea that, being
commons, they were inadequately cultivated. The
main cultivation they have received from the landlords has been of rabbits, grouse, and other game !
The public has been simply played with in the
matter ; and agricultural interests, instead of
being extended and improved, have been severely

damaged. When we realise, in addition to this, that, owing to the increase of the general population and its needs, these tracts which passed into private hands with such slender compensation to the public, are now held up at ruinous prices, we realise that it is high time that the game should cease ; and that the lands which Parliament voted away from the public in those days should now be voted back again—and with " compensation " on a similar scale. These lands are still largely in the hands of the families to whom they were awarded ; and the transfer could perhaps be most fairly and reasonably effected by their simple reversion to the public on the expiration of existing life interests in them. But of course there would have to be land courts to deal with and compensate special cases, as where the land had changed hands, and so forth.

The value of such ancient common lands to the public would now be very great. Large portions of them would be suitable for cultivation and for allocation in small holdings ; the villages would again have a chance of public playgrounds and cricket grounds ; the Parish councils would have lands (so much needed and so difficult to obtain) for allotment gardens ; the District councils might turn many an old woodland into a public park ; while the wilder moors and mountains could be held under County councils or the State, either for afforestation, or as reserves for the enjoyment of the public, and the preservation of certain classes of wild animals and birds, now in danger of extinction.

Let a large measure of this kind be passed retransferring the main portion of the common lands into public hands ; and at the same time a measure compelling owners in the future to declare their land values, and giving power to the public bodies to purchase on the basis of the values so declared ; and already we should have made two important steps towards bringing the land of the nation into the possession of its rightful owners.

VIII

BRITISH ARISTOCRACY AND THE HOUSE
OF LORDS

IT has often been said that our victory at Waterloo
was a great misfortune to England ; and in
general terms the truth of this remark can hardly
be gainsaid. Our successes as against the armies
of the French Revolution certainly kept the current
of new human forces and ideas associated with
that movement at a distance, and warded it off
from our shores. The feudal system, broken down
and disorganised all over the Continent by
Napoleon, preserved its old tradition in these
islands. And one consequence has been that, in
the matters of our Land-system and our Aristocracy, we are now a hundred years behind the
rest of Western Europe.[1]

Our land-system, with its large estates breed-
ing a servile and poor - spirited population of
tenantry and farm laborers, has had the effect
of clogging and depressing British agriculture—
to such a degree, indeed, that the latter has
become a thing despised and neglected by our-

[1] Not to mention our Penal and Civil Codes, so antiquated
and cumbrous compared with the Code Napoleon.

selves and derided by our neighbors. And our Aristocracy has developed to so monstrous and importunate a form that, like some huge parasite, it threatens disease and ruin to the organism upon which it has fastened. It is with the latter trouble that I am at this moment concerned.

It is indeed curious that Britain, which has for so long a time boasted herself in the forefront of human progress, should now be saddled with this institution—a reactionary institution of such magnitude and dead weight as no other nation in the world can show. And more curious still is it that, all the time, with great diligence and apparent zeal, she is enlarging and building up the absurd incubus which weighs her to the ground.

Poor Britain ! with all her other burdens— her burdens of crying poverty, of huge population, of limited land, of distressing fogs both in the mental and physical atmosphere—to be actually fastening and riveting this extra one upon her own back ! What must one think of such a nation? Has she lost her wits, and does she at all divine what she is doing? Is she still lost in a sleep of centuries, and living in dreams of three or four hundred years ago?

There has in the past been a certain glamour and romance about the Feudal Aristocracy. Perhaps distance lends enchantment. We like to lose ourselves in a kind of Tennysonian dream of knights and ladies ; we know that once there were bold bad barons, who certainly were a terrible pest to their contemporaries, but whom we rather admire in the far perspective ; we do not forget the great historical families, whose largesses and whose crimes were on a splendid scale, whose petty jealousies and quarrels with each other were the ruin of peasants and the devastation of country-sides, but whose *noblesse oblige* had elements of heroism and sacrifice in it, even on account of the very fact of its meaning the maintenance of their own Order as against the world. We may readily concede that these people did some work that had to be done, we may allow that there was a certain poetry and creative power in it ; but what has all that to do with the modern Aristocracy?

Of the 550 hereditary peers who to-day constitute the bulk of the House of Lords, it is very doubtful if a single one had a relative present at Runnymede and the signing of the Charter. It is said that only *five* can even trace their families back to that century. In the reign of Elizabeth the lay Lords numbered no more than sixty. Even the Stuarts, who lavished honours on the most dubious favourites, only increased the list of peers by about 100. It was—and the moral is easily drawn—in the reign of George III that the great growth of the modern peerage took place. George himself, anxious to strengthen his weak hand in the Government, insisted on nominating a large contingent—his

congeners and equals in point of brains and education—a crass and fat, snuff-taking and port-
wine-bibbing crew.   William Pitt—and this was
part of his settled policy—drowned out the old
Whig families in the House of Lords " by pouring
into it members of the middle and commercial
class, who formed the basis of his political power
—small landowners, bankers, merchants, nabobs,
army-contractors, lawyers, soldiers, and seamen.
It became the stronghold not of blood, but of
property, the representative of the great estates
and great fortunes which the vast increase of
English wealth was building up." [1]   The whole
process was a sort of strange counterblast to
the French Revolution.   But with Pitt's successors it continued to such an extent that actually
the total number of peerages created during
George the Third's reign was 388 ! [2]

And from that time forward the same.
Britain, to accentuate her victory over Napoleon,
and to assure the world of her anti-revolutionary
principles, steadily added and added to her tale
of titled heads : till now—instead of the feudal
chiefs and royal boon-companions and buccaneers
and sea-dogs of old days—we have a wonderful

[1] J. R. Green, *Short History of the English People*, ch. x.
[2] May's *Constitutional History*, vol. i.   The number of
baronets created during the same reign was 494 ! and of
knights such a crowd that the order has never recovered
from the somewhat aldermanic and provincial flavour it then
acquired.

breccia of brewers and bankers, colliery owners
and Stock Exchange magnates, newspaper proprietors, wine dealers, general manufacturers and
industrial directors, among whom the old landlords lie embedded like fossils.[1]   It must be
confessed that whatever romance a title may have
once carried with it has now quite gone.   It
is hardly possible, one would think, for the most
Philistine Briton or world-foraging Yankee to perceive any glamor in the present aristocracy.
Indeed, one may say that—although, of course, it
includes some very worthy persons—a certain
vulgarity attaches to the class as a whole, and
that it is doubtful whether any really self-respecting commoner would consent to be included in it.

But the curious fact is, as I have said, that
it continues to grow and be added to.   At present
the United Kingdom is blessed with 750 peers
in all (not all of them in the House of Lords),
besides an innumerable host of lesser dignities.
The late Conservative Government, during its ten
years of office, scored fifty-seven additions to the
House—not a bad count ; but Campbell-Banner-
man beat all records by creating twenty in the
course of his first eighteen months !   If the
accretions to the ranks of Rank are to continue
at similar rates, imagination gasps at the probable
situation, say in fifty years.

With regard to this extraordinary freak of
" C.-B.'s," it is difficult to find a rational explana-

[1] Since 1800 the new peers created amount to over 400.

tion, which—in view of the debate at that time
about the sale of honours to wealthy party
supporters—is not also a rather unpleasant one.
In the story of " Bel and the Dragon," when
Daniel determined to destroy the great Idol which
the people worshipped, he fed into its capacious
maw fresh lumps of " pitch and fat and hair "
(of which ingredients, no doubt, the monster was
already composed). He seemed to be nourish-
ing and fattening it, but in reality he destroyed
it, by causing it to " burst in sunder." But
whether the Liberal party really wishes or thinks
to break up the House of Lords in the same way
is extremely doubtful. It is certainly an odd
way of doing battle.

That it can be for a moment supposed that
that House can be converted into a progressive
institution by ample creation of Liberal peers
is out of the question. In the first place, there
is the huge existing Conservative majority there,
to be overcome before anything like a balance
can be established. In the second place, there
is the undeniable and portentous fact that for
turning a man into a Tory, a day in that House
is better than a thousand (outside). For reasons
and in ways not very difficult to see there is a
steady social and conventional pressure going on
in those surroundings, which gradually transforms
well-meaning and progressive folk into rigid ob-
structives. Of the ninety-two peers (and their
successors) created by Liberal Prime Ministers

in the last fifty years, only forty-six, that is one half, are now Liberals.[1] Thirdly, it must be remembered that of those who do thus call themselves Liberals, and under that head are created peers, their real liberality and culture and public spirit (for the most part, and with a few very genuine exceptions) are only skin-deep. They have worked mainly for their own private ends and advancement ; they have been successful men in business or in law ; they have engineered society influences ; they have made themselves grateful to highly placed personages ; they have dumped down enormous funds on occasions for election and other purposes ; they have even obtained what they wanted by forbearing to press for the payment of debts ! In a variety of ways they have been useful to their own side ; and sometimes they have been so little useful that for *that* reason it has been thought better to remove them to " another place." But whatever the cause of their advancement, the end to which it leads will in most cases be the same. It is hard to believe—as Mr. Joseph Clayton says in his excellent little book, *The Truth about the Lords*—that the cause of " temperance legislation will be assisted in the Upper House by Lords Burton and Blyth " ; or that " the progress of labor legislation, in favor of a shorter working day and the abolition of child-labor, will be hastened by Lords Nunburnholme, Pirrie, Glantawe, and

[1] Written in 1908.

Winterstoke." Having climbed the Liberal ladder, the great probability remains that they will scorn the base degrees by which they did ascend, and retire finally to swell the obstructive influences in the Second Chamber.

Lastly—and most important of all—the probability that the House of Lords can be converted into a progressive institution by the creation of Liberal peers is practically *nil,* for the simple reason that the Liberal party itself is not essentially progressive ; and as time goes on gets less and less differentiated in all important respects from the Conservative party—into which in the end it will probably merge.

The whole magnification and bolstering-up of both the House of Lords and the " Aristocracy " generally in this country is certainly an extraordinary phenomenon, and one which would hardly be possible in any other country of the world in this year A.D. Pausing for a moment to take a bird's-eye view of it, and guarding ourselves against undue self-depreciations or too-sweeping comparisons of the Briton with other nations, let us just make a plain matter-of-fact estimate of the situation.

One might suppose that here in the general Aristocracy, among the pick and pink of the nation, endowed with wealth, education, and far-reaching influence, would be found the leaders and pioneers of every great movement ; that art and science, sociology and politics would be illuminated and inspired, organised and marshalled by this class ; that abroad it would stand as representative of what was best and most vigorous in our people ; and that at home and in the country-sides it would set the tone and animate the centres of the most healthy and useful life. What do we actually find? A waste of dullness, commonplaceness and reaction. This Aristocracy does nothing—next to nothing that can be said to be of public utility,[1] for even the really useful work of the ordinary country gentleman on County Councils and as a member of the Great Unpaid can hardly be placed to its account. It produces (in the present day) no artists, no men of letters of any distinction, no inventors, no great men of science, no serious reformers, hardly even a great military general or political leader. And this is certainly astounding when one considers the exceptional opportunities its members have for success and advancement in any of these directions, and the ease with which they can command a hearing and a following.

It is true, of course, that occasionally a man of decided note and ability—a Kelvin or a Tennyson, a Beaconsfield or a Kitchener—on account of real or generally admitted service to the nation, and *not* on account of his swollen

[1] It is nowadays enormously connected among the Directors of Joint Stock Companies and Banks and other money-lending concerns, but whether its labours in these connexions are of public utility is a question

money-bags or his scheming self-advertisement, is collated into the Aristocracy. But such individuals are not numerous, and they are not the *product* of the Aristocracy. They are importations into it which, alas! do not modify its general character, but too often, like good building materials thrown into a swamp, simply sink into it and disappear. The amount of useful genius or talent which the institution, from its hereditary deeps, supplies to the world is an almost negligible quantity.

Again—not to make too great a demand in the way of world-wide genius or service, but to keep to humbler spheres—we may point out that the class in question does not rise to the occasion of its most obvious duties. Despite the efforts of Lord Carrington [1] to arouse its activity, it does not remodel villages on its estates, or create experimental colonies on its broad acres ; it does not meet the very genuine demand now existing for small holdings ; it does not even lend farm lands to Boards of Guardians for the use of the unemployed. If these things have to be tackled, they are left to the generosity and philanthropic zeal of wealthy Americans, who come across the water to polish up the old country. It does not exhibit any pride in making its factories or its quarries or its collieries (where its revenues spring from such sources) models of excellent and cleanly management, with the best

[1] Now (1917) Marquis of Lincolnshire.

conditions possible for the workers concerned in
them. It organises none of the social reforms in
town or country which are so cryingly needed,
and which it ought to be so well qualified to
initiate. It sometimes *appears* (though, of course,
this is not really the fact) as though it could
think of nothing more beneficial for its rural
demesnes and their populations than to shoot over
them, or more appropriate for its town duties
than to employ plenty of dressmakers for
Society functions.

One must not certainly deny that these good
people move up in squadrons, and are greatly
in evidence as Patrons and Patronesses of
Bazaars, or of Hospitals, or of philanthropic
institutions of various kinds. Anything that is
colourless and non-committal, which is popularly
helpful, without being a severe tax on pecuniary
funds or physical energies, and in which a name
or, a title carries weight, is peculiarly favoured.
As Mr. Clayton says (p. 102), " For the laying
of foundation-stones, opening of important buildings, presiding over religious and philanthropic
meetings, the directing of limited liability companies, the ' governing' of self-governing colonies,
and the entertaining of political followers, they
are in great demand." And with all these duties,
and the demands of " Society " generally, it really
would not be fair to call them idle. We may
even say that they are enormously busy.

It would be foolish also to deny—what is

sumciently obvious—that among the titled people, especially the older families, there are found some folk of a humane and cultured class of mind, with charming and genuine good manners, simple habits, and a real sense of responsibility and even affection towards those dependent on them ; and for the existence of such people, in whatever sphere, we may be grateful, especially in these days when they are in danger of being drowned out by tawdry newcomers.

But all this—in the way of benefits or advantages accruing from the Aristocratic system —is very negative. On the other hand, the positive evils of the system do not admit of being overlooked. To the mass of meaningless fashion and expensive idleness created by our social arrangements generally, it accords an *imprimatur* of distinction and desirability. The flagrant sale of high honours—worse, apparently, in the beginning of this twentieth century than ever before —corrupts the nation with the resultant lesson that to make a fortune anyhow and to spend it for personal aggrandisement is the best way to gain distinction and public respect. Trafficking in titles has become quite a profession, and a rich man has now little difficulty, through the mediation of diplomatic but impecunious ladies of rank, in getting himself made a knight or a baronet. A quite uncalled-for and disproportionate power is put into the hands of persons who are really not worthy of it, whose aims are vulgar, whose education is poor, on whose tables hardly a book of real merit is to be found (often, certainly, not as good literature as is seen in a better-class workman's home) ; and among whom the questions most important to be discussed are whether golf or motoring, baccarat or bridge, shall be the order of the day.   Gangs of similar folk use their " influence " to get important positions in Army or Navy or official circles filled up by relatives or favorites ; and the resultant scandals of incompetence or maladministration, which later years inevitably unfold, are hushed up by the same influences.   The nation is heavily injured, but the damage does not recoil on the heads of those most responsible.   " Society " twaddle fills the newspapers and impresses the uninitiated and unlearned ; the aimless life and ideals silting downwards infect the masses of the people with a most futile and feeble conception of life ; and in little matters of dress and etiquette ultimately make the middle classes even worse than those whom they imitate, and from whom they suppose the fashions to originate.

To return to the House of Lords. I have no intention here of dwelling on its record of inefficiency and obstruction.   Of its political history during the last century ; of its meagre and scanty attendances, even over the most important questions ; of its marvelous inefficiency and want of comprehension in dealing with the same ; of its indifference when any human or humane inte-

rest has been concerned ; of its dead obstructive-
ness when such things seemed to endanger in any
degree its " rights of property " ; of its clinging
to the death-penalty (in 1810) for the stealing
of values over 5s., and to the same (in 1820)
for values over £10, and to the same again (in
1839) for sheep-stealing ; of its maintenance by
large majorities of vivisection (1879), and of
trap pigeon-shooting (1883) ; of its turning deaf
ears to the pleading cry of children in the coal
mines (1842), or of little chimney-sweep urchins
in the chimneys (1849), or of evicted and famine-
stricken peasants in Ireland (1880-2) ; of its
steady refusal, until fairly forced, to grant the
rightful and natural demands of citizens for
suffrage and self-government and religious equality
and the education of their boys and girls ; or
to grant the demands of women for rights over
their own property and persons, and of men for
the protection of their own labor-power ;—are
not all these things written in the great books
of the Chronicles of the last hundred years, as
well as in the pages of the Almanacks and the
manifestos of the late Mr. Stead?   There is only
one opinion about them ; and what has been
said a thousand times it is needless to repeat.

Nor can we fairly expect anything else.   If
we indulge in the absurdity and scandal of making
men high legislators because they have heaped
together huge fortunes by selling " purge " and
" kill-devil " to a drink-sodden public, or have

made themselves wealthy and notorious by circulating lying and sensation-mongering *canards* among ignorant populations, we must expect the absurdities and scandals and misfortunes which are the logical result. And if it only stopped there ! But to go further, and to make the bodily *heirs* of these people our future High Legislators, even to the crack of doom—well, that is surely midsummer madness, and a gilding of the refined gold of folly ! As a precise and practical writer has remarked : " Our toleration of this costly absurdity is the wonder of the world. Its like is not to be found in any other civilised nation."

The real question which remains is, What is to be the cure? Dismissing the supposition that a syndicate of American millionaires will buy up the House of Lords complete for the purposes of a world-exhibition, and, on the other hand, the supposition that a violent wave of socialist revolution will drown it suddenly out of existence— as being, both of them, though feasible, beyond the range of immediate politics, we may at least, and as a practical issue, discuss what considerable and radical changes would really bring this institution, and that of the Aristocracy generally, into the line of human usefulness. There is fair reason to suppose that in a few years the Labor party or parties in the Lower House will have a decisive influence there ; and in view of that probability some suggestions for a future policy

with regard to the Peers may be useful—though
the following proposals (it must be understood)
are merely individual, and would not perhaps
be accepted in block by any of the Socialist
organisations.

I think we may assume that, short of a
violent catastrophe, the Second Chamber will be
retained. Its total abolition would not be in
accordance with the temper and tradition of the
British ; and, personally, I think that—as long as
our present general Constitution remains—a
Second Chamber is desirable ; because our
House of Commons—though with an intelligent
voting public it might *become* intelligent, and even
get to know a little political economy—must
always, from the method of its election, be largely
composed of professional politicians, and must
represent mainly popular ideals, views, and
currents of opinion. There is no harm in this,
but it requires to be corrected by a more searching, accurate, and experienced spirit (if only, for
example, in order that Bills passed by the popular
Assembly may be intelligible, and may not become
law while still containing hopelessly contradictory
clauses). Also a Chamber with some intelligent
and public-spirited initiative about it would be
very helpful.

A Second Chamber, then, seems to me on the
whole advisable, and will, I have no doubt, for
a long time to come be demanded by the

British people. It will not necessarily be the House of Lords ; but here again the British love of tradition and continuity will come in, and will probably insist on its being *called* the House of Lords—even long after it has come to consist mainly of manual workers and advanced women !

The practical question therefore is—how to begin immediately to remodel the Upper House with a view to rendering it (in time) a useful Second Chamber.

The first and immediate need obviously is to drop the hereditary qualification. No son of an existing peer should sit in a future House simply on account of being an eldest son. He may succeed to his father's title (of that more anon), but not therefore to his father's seat. The present House will not be wiped out, but in the twinkling of an eye it will be changed, as far as its legislative functions are concerned, to a body of life-peers. The descendants of the existing peers will (possibly) carry on their ornamental functions in Society, but they will cease to be our hereditary Legislators. This is so very indispensable a reform, and the scandal and absurdity of the present arrangement is so monstrous, that without making this first step practically nothing can be done ; and the public must simply choose between this and eternal disgrace. Moreover, it is a reform which could be carried out almost imperceptibly, and with a minimum of friction.

The present House would remain, for the

moment, undissolved ; but its numbers would slowly dwindle with the decease of its members. All future peers created in order to supply the consequent vacancies would be life-peers. Whatever other titles they might carry, or if they carried no titles at all, in either case their right to sit in the House would not descend to their offspring. Thus in the course of not so very many years we should have a Second Chamber wholly consisting of life - members appointed on their own merits, and neither claiming nor exercising hereditary power.[1]

What would be the general principles of appointment to such a Chamber? It might be urged that (after it was once fairly established) it should be made self-elective—say like the Chinese Academy, which for more than a thousand years has exercised so tremendous a sway over

---

[1] Lord Hobhouse, in 1894, proposed such a Second Chamber, limited to 200 or 250 life-members, and having also a limited right of veto (*Contemporary Review*, December 1894). Sir Herbert Maxwell proposed that the Crown should cease to grant hereditary titles, and should be content with creating life-peerages ; also that the number of members of the Upper House should be reduced to 268 (*Nineteenth Century*, July 1906). Mr. Frederic Harrison has sketched a similar Senate, drawn widely from the various professions, learned societies, and so forth (*Positivist Review*, October 1906). Constitutionally, the peers are summoned by the Will of the Crown, and apart from that have no hereditary right to sit, and on the other hand it is amply admitted now that the Crown has power to grant peerages and summon peers for life only ; so we see that the change proposed would involve no great technical or constitutional difficulty.

the destiny of China.   As every one knows, the
Chinese Academy consists of some 240 members,
the best scholars and *savants* in the empire, to
each of whom by immemorial provision is allowed
a house and a small salary.   The duty of the
body is to debate and turn its critical acumen
and enlightenment on any or every public question
that may arise.   It has no direct legislative or
executive power ; but the results of its debates
and its recommendations are widely circulated
through the empire, and have an immense influence
on the popular mind, while at the same time the
body exercises or has exercised a very outspoken
censorship over the acts of officials and even of
the Emperor himself.   This body is self-elective.
When a vacancy occurs the remaining members
elect the new one.   It is thus independent of
patronage, and no doubt (as the remarkable history
of the Chinese Academy shows), when once a
good tradition is started, this method of election
may be very effective.

With regard to the House of Lords, however,
there might (at present) be objections to this
method—and we may take it as probable that
new (life) peers will continue to be created, and
writs of summons issued, on the recommendation
of the Premier at the time in office.   Assuming
this, I think it must follow, as the second absolutely necessary reform, that in all cases a reason
(of distinguished service) must be given for each
creation.   Sir Wilfrid Lawson on one occasion,

in 1887 I believe, proposed this. And it is clear that to leave the distribution of high honours and the position of Hereditary National Legislator to the irresponsible appointment of any Government, is simply to court bribery, corruption, and malversation. A distinct and sufficient reason must be given for each creation, just as is done in the case of the award of a medal or decoration, a V.C. or a D.S.O. ; and though this in itself might not always secure the best men, it would certainly go a long way to keep out the commonplace and really harmful types, whose real recommendation to-day consists in services which would not bear public scrutiny. Of course this reform will be strenuously resisted by certain classes, just for the very reason that irresponsible patronage is so dear and so very convenient to those who can exercise it ; but the change is absolutely necessary and indispensable.

It would probably have to be accompanied by some indication as to the kind of distinguished service which should be regarded as a qualification. Personally, I think that in this Second Chamber, or House of Life-peers, as far as possible, *every* class or section of the nation should be represented, and represented of course by well-known and well-tried members of such class, or by those who have done good service to their class or to the nation. Lord Rosebery, in 1884, in moving for a Select Committee on the reform of the House of Lords, " specified nine classes which were entirely without representation in that House. The first were the Nonconformists, the last the Workmen. The other seven were as follows—medicine, science, literature, commerce, tenant-farmers, arts, and colonists. He suggested that life-peers should be created, and that the ancient system of assistants, by which judges were called into council, might be revived." [1]   Here, at any rate, as far as it went, was a practical suggestion towards making the House an efficient and useful body. But the details of such membership, *ex officio* and other, would of course need careful consideration, and into that question we need not go now. What is clear, at present, is that the future House of Peers (and here the word " peers " comes in very appropriately) will consist of able men of *all* classes and so-called ranks in society. And this is in the line of a very obvious and natural evolution. In early times the Lords Spiritual, who often outnumbered the Lords Temporal in the House, were not a little jealous of the latter. Towards the close of the eighteenth century the old landed families, who alone beside the Church were there represented, were furiously disgusted at the accession to their ranks of large bodies of commercial and professional gentry. Again, in 1856, there was a storm in the House over the granting of a

[1] W. T. Stead, *Peers or People : An Appeal to History*, p. 194, 1907.

life-peerage to Lord Wensleydale ; the highest legal and historical authorities, however, maintained that it was the ancient right and privilege of the Crown to create life-peers ; and in 1887 the Appellate Jurisdiction Act was passed, in accordance with which certain Law-lords now take their seats for life *ex officio*. Finally, in the last twenty years, classes of men have been admitted to the House whom even George III would not have dared to propose. Sir Erskine May, in his *Constitutional History of England*, speaking of the great growth in numbers of the Upper House in modern times, says : " With this large increase of numbers the peerage has undergone further changes no less remarkable, in its character and composition. It is no longer a council of the magnates of the Land—the territorial Aristocracy, the descendants or representatives of the barons of the olden time ; but in each successive age it has assumed a more popular and representative character." Thus, although the present House would, no doubt, be much shocked at the idea, it does not seem at all improbable that a time may come when a Joseph Arch, for instance, as an eminent farm-laborer and representative of farm-laborers, might be called to sit on its councils.

Another reform which will probably be advisable will be the limitation of the new House of Life-peers to a definite number of members

—although, of course, such limiting number might be alterable from time to time. One great advantage of such a limitation is, that on any occasion the number of vacancies existing is known, and the question of their replenishment comes naturally before the public, so that, whoever the appointing authority may be, he or they cannot easily act in a secret or underhand way in the matter, as is indeed too possible with the present method.

The reforms thus proposed are practically three :—

1. Life-peerages (the actual title a matter of little importance).

2. Adequate reasons of useful service to be given for each creation—on democratic grounds more or less scheduled and recognised.

3. Limitation of number of members.

Under such conditions as these reforms would induce, the Second Chamber would probably turn out satisfactorily, and there does not seem any reasons why its powers should be seriously curtailed. To propose to keep the House of Lords as it is, is practically to *ask* for the curtailment of its powers and the suspension of the right of veto—for it is evident that things cannot go on very long as they are ; but to remove the right of veto would in effect be to reduce the House to a mere revising body—whose work could, of course, be better done by a committee of experts. If a Second Chamber is to be retained at all, far more sensible would it be to make it a really useful and intelligent institution, with power of initiative and power of veto—the latter at any rate to some degree, though of course guarded. Short of our securing such useful and intelligent body, Abolition would be the only alternative.

There remain a few words to say about the Aristocracy generally, and the possibilities of bringing it into line as a serviceable or even tolerable institution. It is fairly clear that the same arguments which have been brought forward in favor of a life-seat only in the House of Peers, and in favor of a declaration of the reasons for conferring that distinction, apply equally—though not perhaps equally pressingly —to the conferring of titles generally. Of course, it would be possible to raise a man to a baronage or an earldom, and in doing so to give him a life-seat only in the Second Chamber, while at the same time continuing his *title* to his heirs ; but the question arises, Why—because a man has done useful service to the nation (assuming, of course, that he has), and the nation to show its gratitude confers some title upon him—why should the irresponsible heirs of this man, and of other such men, be allowed *in perpetuo* to sport similar titles, and so to form (as we see) a class of

Society idlers (or busybodies) who, to say the least, exercise an enfeebling and unworthy influence on the rest of the people?[1] It may be replied to that, that as long as you take from such folk direct legislative power, the thing does not matter. If any such classes like to whirl round in their little coteries, and have their smart dinner-parties and their scandals, their punctilios of precedence and their privileges of heading lists of subscriptions, why should the nation interfere to deprive them of these simple pleasures? And there is so far truth in this, that we must admit that as long as the present commercial system continues, and there remains, as to-day, a sum of some 600 millions sterling of *unearned* income, or more, to be divided every year among the capitalist and landlord classes, this feeble and unworthy life *will* probably continue among such classes, whether titled or not. That is so far true ; but it forms no reason why the nation, by a system of rank without service, should give its *imprimatur* of distinction to such a life.

Again, there may be some people who believe in Blood so far as to think that the descendants of a really great man inherit his virtues to a remote posterity. And it certainly seems possible

---

[1] It should also be pointed out that if it is desired to confer distinction by titles, the latter *must* be for life only —since the hereditary system gives no distinction, no distinction between authentic genius and the commonplace wearer of a family coronet.

that some day—when there is a State department of Eugenics—whole families may be granted
a pedigree and diploma on account of their excellent breed ; but then I need hardly say that such
patent of nobility would be immediately cancelled
for any person who should breed children outside
the regulation of the State—as I fear many of
our aristocracy at present do ! And as to the
Blood descending *with the Name*, a very brief
calculation will dispel that illusion, for it is easily
found (doubling at each generation) that *ten*
generations back one had over a thousand
ancestors living (say in 1600 A.D.), while ten
generations again before that (say in 1300) one
had over a *million*. Any one, therefore, who
can trace his descent from some ancestor living
in 1300—and there are few indeed who can do
that—will have the satisfaction of knowing that
one-millionth [1] part of the blood in his veins
will be due to that ancestor !

I have referred—in speaking of the House of
Lords—to the Chinese Academy, which seems an
extraordinarily practical and sensible institution.
We might do worse than take a hint from China
as to the handling of titles generally. Greatly
and devoutly as John Chinaman believes in
heredity, descent, and ancestor-worship, he is not

[1] It is true that, according to the Mendelian theory of
heredity, there may occasionally emerge a very near replica
of some fairly remote ancestor ; but, as I say, it will in all
probability be of an ancestor *not* in the line of the Name.

such a fool as to close his eyes to the fact
that blood very soon runs out and becomes inter-
mixed.   Chester Holcombe, for some years Acting
Minister of the United States at Peking, says of
the Chinese in his excellent book, *The Real Chinaman* : " There is no titled nobility, with its long
list of elder and younger sons, sons-in-law, and
cousins near and remote, to be supported from
the public funds, and to fill all the more important positions of honor and profit.   The few
titles that are from time to time bestowed carry
nothing with them but the nominal honor ;
they are bestowed as rewards for distinguished
services, and have never been recognised as
forming the basis of any claim whatever upon
either offices or treasury.   In a way they are
hereditary, but soon run out, *since the rank de-
creases one grade with each generation.*   Even
the imperial clan forms no exception to this rule.
The author has many a time had in his employ
a man who, as a relative of the Emperor, was
entitled to wear the imperial yellow girdle ; but
he was a hod-carrier, and earned six cents a
day."

With this suggestion—for the benefit of some
future Government — I will close.   Let our
Aristocracy, as far as it is hereditary, be " let
down gently " by the rank descending one grade
with each generation.   This already happens with
the younger children of our higher ranks, who

receive courtesy titles for life.   Let a system of such courtesy titles be extended for two or three generations, and let all children in that respect count as younger children ; and in a few years we should have got rid of a foolish and somewhat vulgar anachronism.

IX

SOCIAL AND POLITICAL LIFE IN CHINA[1]

I

IN speaking of China, it is necessary to guard against a misconception still greatly current, namely that the Chinese are a backward, ignorant nation, slumbering in a kind of agelong lethargy. In many respects this notion is the reverse of the truth. In many respects the Chinese are the most wide-awake of races. They are certainly one of the most remarkable. Intelligent, observant, accurate, industrious, kindly, polite, tenacious of custom, having an immense history stretching back thousands of years, they are at once among the oldest and the most childlike of peoples—old and wise in the accumulated experience of their own past, yet little more than children in face of some of the problems which to-day the West presents to them. It is only in the latter sense that any awakening of China can be spoken of or expected.

Their historical records come down in a con-

[1] Originally published as an article in *The Co-operative Annual* (1907).

tinuous stream from some 4,000 years ago ; [1]
and, though there has been constant development during that time, there has been no great
break in their institutions. There is no record
of a time when they did not occupy the country
they now occupy ; no record of a time when they
had not a monarchical system, in general outline
the same as they now possess [2]—never a time
when the great masses of the people were not
agricultural as now, never a time when they were
not practically self-sufficing and independent of
other countries and peoples. Time and time again
they have been invaded. Tartars, Manchurians,
Mahommedans, Christians, Japanese, Dutch, Portuguese, English, and Russians have poured in
upon them ; yet they have never been very
greatly disturbed. With a smile that is childlike
and bland John Chinaman has pursued the even
tenor of his way. And his teeming millions,
instead of being conquered, have simply
swallowed up the invader and continued much
as before.

Printing, as is well known, was invented in
China 500 years before it was used in Europe ;
gunpowder even before that—though it shows
sadly for the intelligence of the Chinese that

[1] There is a document preserved in the Shoo-king or Book
of History which seems to be an actual survey of the kingdom as it existed in the twenty-third century B.C.

[2] No essential modification can at any period in all the
centuries be discovered in their system of government.—
Holcombe, *The Real Chinaman*, p. 31.

they did not use it for killing people with till
they were taught by the Europeans'!¹   Their
astronomical observations are among the oldest
in the world, dating some 2,000 years B.C.   As
much as seventeen or eighteen hundred years
ago they adopted changes of a socialist character,
and began to establish their land system on a
reasonable basis.   Seven or eight hundred years
ago they tried the use of an irredeemable paper
currency, and found it wanting ²   And for centuries past (till quite recently) the military
profession has been lapsing into contempt and
disuse as unworthy of a great people.

After these considerations it is not very
surprising to find that this great nation coming
down from the remote past found itself in the
early centuries of our era—or at any rate had
good reason to think itself—the most advanced
and civilised on the whole earth.   We read that
Marcus Antoninus in A.D. 166 sent an embassy
by sea to China to procure the rich silks which
that country produced.   The culture of silk was
brought thence into Europe during the Emperor
Justinian s reign.   Tea plants were carried from
India to China in A.D. 315, and Chinese physi-
cians and Chinese engineers were employed in

---

¹ By the Portuguese, early in the seventeenth century.
² It drove the metallic currency out of the country.   See
The Real Chinese Question, by Chester Holcombe (Methuen,
1901), p. 231 ; also a careful history of the paper currency in
China, in *Primitive Civilisations*, vol. ii, ch. xvi.

Persia in the twelfth and thirteenth centuries.[1]
From that period onwards its experiences of
other peoples were not very favorable. French,
Portuguese, Spaniards, Dutch, Russians, and
Britons appeared in turn, but their conduct was
more that of pirates than of civilised men. More
and more did the Celestial Empire learn to look
on all outsiders as ' barbarians ' and ' foreign
devils.' More and more it shut itself away from
the world. It established a ring-fence about
itself, and lived in isolated superiority. It
remained sublimely ignorant of the rise of the
great Western nations, and of what we call
modern Progress ; and so came about the extraordinary result that in 1835 or so, a little before
our Opium war with China, that ancient nation,
from Emperor to peasant, was living in pro-
foundest ignorance of what we call Modern Civilisation ; in sublime, celestial, and indeed quite
ludicrous sense of its own superiority over " the
red-haired, green-eyed, hairy-faced monsters of
the West, with feet one cubit and two-tenths
long," who were supposed to inhabit Europe ; and
in the sharpest possible contrast to them, both
of life and ideals.[2]

[1] See *China* (Bohn Series), p. 19.
[2] It is even now commonly supposed in China that the
European missionaries dig out the eyes of children in their
schools, and, pounding them with other ingredients in a
mortar, make of them a magic paste of infernal potency.
It was this superstition that led to the awful Tientsin massacre
in 1870.

It may be that our ignorance of China is in reality little less remarkable than theirs concerning us. We most of us think we know something about the subject. We have relations or friends who have been along the Coast, and who have brought back outlandish tales ; we have read similar accounts in the columns of the daily Press ; but such things hardly touch the fringe of the matter. In all such cases where along a seaboard one race or civilisation comes into direct contact with another race and civilisation the result is—just what one might expect—a disorganisation and corruption of *both*. Probably there are few more corrupt *European* populations than those you find at Hongkong, Shanghai, and the other ports along that coast. And, on the other hand, the Chinese populations in those places give you no more just idea of the great interior of China than a stroll down Ratcliffe Highway and the London Docks would give you of British home life and industry. The mass of books and print dealing with China describe this motley, mongrel, and degenerate civilisation of the seaboard. Nevertheless there is a literature dealing with the true Interior, and sufficient, at any rate with a little study—and with plentiful allowance for dark patches (as for superstitions, cruelties, ignorance, poverty, famines, etc)—to give us a glimpse of a vast ocean of population, not to be counted at much less than 400,000,000, and probably the most stable, the most well-rooted, the most content, equal, agricultural and peace-loving on the whole earth.[1]

This may sound too strongly worded ; but, in order to show that there is some foundation for the view, I will first quote a few general remarks by well-known and reliable authorities on the subject, and then proceed to a more detailed account.

Professor Giles, in his *Historic China and Sketches*, says (p. 124) : " Food and lodging are cheap in China, and it may be roundly stated that every man, woman, and child has something in the way of clothes, two full meals a day, and a shelter at night " ; also, " The normal state of the people of China is one of considerable pros-perity and great natural happiness." Fortune, in his *Residence among the Chinese*, says : " I doubt if there is a happier race anywhere than the Chinese farmers and peasantry " ; and A. J.

[1] Some of the best books on this subject are :—*The Middle Kingdom*, by S. Wells Williams, 2 vols. (New York, 1883) ; *Primitive Civilisations*, by E. J. Simcox (Sonnenschein, 1894), vol. ii ; *La Cite Chinoise*, by Eugène Simon (Paris, 1894) ; *Historic China and Sketches*, by Professor H. A. Giles; *The Real Chinaman*, by Chester Holcombe (Hodder & Stoughton, 1895) ; *The Real Chinese Question*, by Chester Holcombe (Methuen, 1900); *" These from the Land of Sinim,"* by Sir Robert Hart (Chapman & Hall, 1901) ; *China's Only Hope*, by the Viceroy Chang Chih Tung (Oliphant, Anderson, & Ferrier, 1901) ; *China in Transformation*, by A. R. Colquhoun (Harper Bros., 1898) ; *Intimate China*, by Mrs. A. J. Little ; and *Village and Town Life in China*, by Y. K. Leong and L. K. Tao (Allen & Unwin, 1915).

Little in *Through the Yangtse Gorges* : " Riches
are fairly distributed, and the contrast of grinding poverty with arrogant wealth, which is the
rule in Europe, is the exception here."

I will now sketch out very roughly some of
the leading ideas and institutions of the Chinese
polity, premising of course that over a country
so vast as China, with its various climates, races,
dialects, etc., there is necessarily a considerable
variation in details ; [1] also that my object is
not to excite an ignorant attention by the recital
of wonders and absurdities, nor to flatter our own
complacency by dwelling on the follies or failures
of a distant civilisation, but to point out the
great constructive lines and inspirations of that
civilisation (surely one of the most remarkable
in the world) ; and then to pass on to a consideration of what great changes are likely to
ensue both in itself and abroad owing to its
contact with the civilisations of the West.

One of the most salient, and to us most
interesting, characteristics of China is the essential Democracy of its institutions, and the sense

[1] It is interesting, however, to find that writers agree on
the essential homogeneity of the Chinese people. Chester
Holcombe says : " History furnishes no parallel of any race
or nation of noticeable size so homogeneous, so uniform,
and so intense in its characteristics. Their nationality is
burned into them. They cannot slough it off or exchange
it for any other. They absorb other races. But they remain
always Chinese."—*The Real Chinese Question*, p. 96. See also
Primitive Civilisations, vol. ii, p. 290.

and practice of Equality among its populations. Unlike India, we may almost say that there is no hereditary class or caste in China. The only caste is the Literary Caste, from which all officials are taken, and admission to this (by examination) is so free and open that the ascent of a boy of the poorest family to the highest positions and honours is quite usual and excites no special notice. Eugene Simon, whose knowledge of China is most intimate, asserts (*La Cite Chinoise,* p. 62) that it is rare to find a family, however lowly, which has not some member, close or distant, of highest rank ; and that owing to this perpetual rise and fall in station the whole population is leavened through with the sentiment of equality ; and of course, correspondingly, with the sense of its own dignity. While Chester Holcombe, in *The Real Chinese Question* (p. 62), goes so far as to say that " during many centuries the heads of the Government, always excepting the Emperor, have commonly been the sons of poor unknown parents."

In all countries class divisions create arrogance, insolence, servility, and boorishness. In China a necessary result of the general sense of equality is good manners. Nothing is more cultivated than politeness. Even the beggar must be treated with the respect due to a perfect gentleman. And it is said that the early Christian missionaries, accustomed to the behavior of carters in their own Western lands—where, if two met in a narrow lane, they would often fall to violent language and sometimes to blows—were astonished to see Chinamen in a similar situation bowing to each other with the utmost deference, and apologising profusely for getting in each other's way !

Again, this sense of equality and good manners is closely connected with the whole manner of life of these vast populations. There is no country in the world where a large population is spread out over the land in secure cultivation of innumerable small holdings, and in modest family independence and prosperity, to a like degree as in China. Everything in Chinese history is ancient, and at an early period the phases, first of the village commune and then of the agglomeration of lands into private hands, were passed through. The evils of the latter state of affairs were realised, and many laws and regulations were adopted for the purpose of checking the growth of large estates and of a landless class. Among these was a special tax on arable land not cultivated,[1] doubtless with the object of discouraging indolent ownership. And the result of all these measures and movements, extending over many centuries, has been that, at the present time, not only is it most rare for any one to own or occupy more than, say, 250 acres, but there is an unwritten law of

[1] See *Primitive Civilisations*, vol. ii, p. 50,

public opinion which makes it discreditable to do so, or to live upon the rents of land without being actually engaged in their cultivation.[1] The State from the very earliest times has exercised a kind of overlordship over the lands and assessed a tax upon them, which in the present day runs to about 20d. to 22d. per acre.[2] Subject to this tax a family is perfectly secure in its tenure, or may rent out portions of its land to others—a thing not infrequently done as a matter of convenience between *bona-fide* cultivators, though not approved of on such a scale as would lead to mere landlordism.

The consequence of all this is that all the more productive parts of China—the plains of the great rivers and the slopes of the lower hills—present to-day a scene of extraordinary fertility and of widespread democratic industry. For hundreds of miles together the land is covered by an immense patchwork or network of small holdings—of an average size, perhaps, of five or six acres, and rarely exceeding fifty acres—running together into small hamlets or clusters of cottages, each with their school or meeting house, their wells and lift-pumps worked by buffaloes, their tanks

[1] Simon, *La Cité Chinoise*, p. 37.
[2] Rev. A. Williamson, *Journeys in Northern China*, 1870, p. 167. Professor S. Wells Williams says it varies from 20 to 66 cents (say 10d. to 2s. 9d.) per acre, according to quality of land, etc. (*The Middle Kingdom*, vol. i, p. 294). The revenue of China, except for a small amount in likin dues and Customs, is entirely derived from the Land Tax.

and irrigation channels. Here are grown crops of the most varied and valuable kind—tea-bushes planted in orderly lines and patches, groves of oranges, clumps of bamboo or sugar cane, verdant squares of young rice, pollard mulberries for the silkworms, plots of cotton and maize and wheat and yam and clover, not to mention less known things like wax trees and varnish trees. John Chinaman, as is well known, is about the best agriculturist in the world. For centuries and centuries the country has been face to face with the problem of supporting its immense population off its own lands, and though necessarily at times and places, in seasons of drought or social disturbance, the pressure of population on the means of subsistence produces frightful famines and widespread distress, yet, on the whole, the manner in which this problem is solved is the admiration of all observers. Simon gives very detailed and interesting accounts of the Chinese agricultural methods, and says it is not uncommon for a Chinaman to obtain five or six crops in a year off one plot of ground.[1]

Over all this land may be seen the silver threads of irrigation-canals and ditches, skirting the hills for scores and hundreds of miles—often three or four tiers of them one above another—and serpentining down to the lower slopes and plains. Irrigation for thousands of years has been one of the main public objects, and

[1] *La Cité Chinoise*, pp. 304, 305.

innumerable public or private efforts and bene-
factions have enriched the country with its
present complete system, without which of course
its agriculture could not be carried on. The
larger canals too form waterways for boats and
traffic, and the hamlets, villages, and occasional
large towns are knit together by innumerable
footpaths and a few but not many highroads
for wheel traffic. Of this industrial and commercial life we read ⊢—

> China is one great hive of commerce. Every part is
> reached from every other part. The whole business certainly
> is done under the most antiquated, cumbersome, and expen-
> sive methods, and with an enormous waste of time. But it
> is done. The inns everywhere are full of business travelers.
> The rivers and canals are crowded with cargo-carrying craft
> of every description, and bound in every direction. The
> roads and mountain passes are clamorous with the shouts
> and calls of drivers of camels, drivers of horses, mules, and
> donkeys, and with porters of every age and both sexes, all
> loaded to the extreme limit of endurance with every name-
> able class or description of goods, bound for a market.
> There are native banks of exchange in every city of size,
> by means of which money may be safely remitted to any
> part of China, however remote. And, in addition to the
> Government service of couriers, there are postal and express
> companies which transmit letters and parcels everywhere.[1]

But the cultivation and occupation of the Land
is the main thing. Every family in China desires
to be rooted in the land—to have a few acres
of its own, a family burial place, and a spot
sacred to ancestor-worship. Though folk emi-

[1] *The Real Chinese Question*, p. 328.

grate to the towns (and towns of a million population are not so rare), still, it is but for a
time. The great object is to make a little money,
purchase a plot, and establish oneself and descendants on the land.

Thus one great root of Chinese life is the
Land. The other is the Family. And I must
give a few lines to the family.

The family in China does not mean quite the
same as with us. It is a term of wider import.
It not only means man and wife and their
children, but it often also includes married sons
and their wives and children, and may also include
brothers of the man and their families and
descendants. It largely goes with the land.
When a younger son marries he may stay on with
his wife and young family in the household of
his father ; but as soon as he can afford it he
will generally obtain a plot of land for himself
and plant himself out (since his elder brother or
brothers will remain on the ancestral plot). He
will thus found a new family or ancestral branch,
and secure a place where his own memory
and presence may be kept green and sacred.
Ancestor-worship lies at the back of the whole
life of China and of Japan ; but it is a very
difficult thing for us Westerners to understand.
It is not at all what we at first think—namely
a pious respect paid to the virtue and character
of a predecessor—or at least it is something
much *more*, and more intimate, than that. It

is a very real sense of the *presence* of that ancestor, and of his or her continued life within and around the living person. He (or she) is here still, though unseen, is looking out of our eyes, hearing with our ears, is moving and working and influencing events in our neighborhood.[1] Hundreds, thousands of the dead surround us. We shall in time join their company.[2] All life is given a kind of sacredness through this cause.

The Chinaman sets apart a room for the worship of his forbears. If he is too poor to afford a whole room, he still sets apart one end of a room. There, on shelves, are placed the memorial tablets of his ancestors, or of deceased members of his family. On a table in front flowers are placed, and on occasions incense is burnt. Here he comes to meditate ; and here, once a fortnight or once a month, is held the family conclave or meeting.

This is a weighty affair, and holds an important place not only in the life of the Family, but of the Nation. As we have said, the family group may form a numerous body. The

[1] See Lafcadio Hearn in *Kokoro*, p. 270 : " To Japanese thought the dead are not less real than the living. They take part in the daily life of the people—sharing the humblest sorrows and the humblest joys."

[2] It will be remembered that General Nogi in the Russo-Japanese War addressed the spirits of the dead soldiers, informing them of the late victories, and thanking them for their co-operation.

members gather together, dressed in holiday attire. The head of the family—who is generally of course a man, but occasionally a widowed mother or grandmother — conducts a sort of service. There is an invocation to Heaven and to the spirits of the departed ancestors ; and then, turning to the table in the centre of the room, the head of the family opens the record book—in which all family events and histories have been inscribed—and reads from it the life of some one or other of the ancestors or predecessors ; changing of course each time, so that in the course of two or three years the younger members of the family become quite familiar with the histories of those who have gone before them, and can surely profit by them for encouragement or warning. The history having been read, the head of the house goes on to fill up the book to date from the last meeting with the events which have happened in the interval —the births, deaths, marriages, and lesser happenings—and then the meeting resolves itself into a sort of tribunal to pass judgment, if necessary, on the actions of the various members.

This is a very important and very interesting function of the family assembly, and it has a bearing far beyond the immediate life of the family, for it in reality takes the place and does most of the work of our magistrates and police courts. In China the honor of the family is of the most sacred character, and is upheld before all things, To strike a father or mother is punishable by death—whatever the provocation may be. And anything which tarnishes or slurs the family name is resented to the highest degree. The family therefore keeps the strictest watch upon its own members ; and if at any monthly meeting there is an accusation lying against a member—perhaps preferred by some neighboring family—as of quarrel, or theft, or any misdemeanor, this is gone into with punctilious care ; and the relative is either cleared or, if found guilty, punished by his own people ! (the punishment may be a fine, or even blows, and, in quite extreme cases, expulsion from the family.) So careful are families in these proceedings, and so great is their sense of public honor, that it appears that in the proceedings of the public and higher courts of the land an entry in a family record book as to any matter of fact is taken as sufficient proof and evidence of that fact—the falsification of a record book being a thing almost unknown and unthought of.

According to Simon, one of the first questions asked when the meeting resolves itself into a tribunal is whether every member has duly paid his taxes ! and this to us forms a very impressive testimony to their sense of civic honor. Certainly, the institution of the family meeting must produce a great impression on the children, who are thus brought up in an atmosphere alive with the consciousness of public duty and respon-

sibility. And the schools work in the same
direction. Their teaching as regards anything
resembling science or matters of fact is lamentably
bad and absurd, and as regards literature and
manners it is overloaded with petty rules and
regulations ; but as regards the general Confucian principles of justice and sincerity, straight-
forward dealing, and duty to neighbor and State,
it is quite excellent, and indeed superior to *our*
school teaching, which for the most part ignores
these things. It may be in consequence of this
that the standard of public honesty in China is
really very high—though this fact is not always
admitted by us, and a good deal of official corruption (which certainly exists) is quoted to prove
the contrary. Our merchants, however, all agree
that the Chinese trader is most reliable to deal
with, and that his word is as good as his bond.

The family tribunal—by thus at one stroke, as
it were, sweeping off the cases that come before
our petty courts—disposes of a vast number
of evils which fester round our police-courts and
police system. Police are reduced to a minimum, and are almost non-existent in the country
districts.[1] The public courts are few in number,[2]

[1] "That crime is not very rife in China is sufficiently shown
by their having no police force."—Mrs. Archibald Little in
Intimate China, p. 140.

"A sort of village police is maintained in some districts by
the inhabitants under the authority of the village elder."—
S. Wells Williams, *Middle Kingdom*, vol. i, p. 483.

[2] The Abbe Huc, in his *Chinese Empire* (vol. ii, ch. vii),

and have only the more serious cases to deal
with, often those in which the criminals concerned
have been expelled from their families ; and
though the methods of the courts are summary
and often barbaric, yet it is a query whether on
the whole they are so much worse than ours.[1]

The results of all this on the national life—of
the widespread sense and practice of Equality, of
the rooting of so vast a population in the Land,
of its rooting in the Family, with its own indi-
genous tribunals, rites, and customs—is to produce
a social organisation extraordinarily simple and
stable, though loosely compacted, and a people
more thoroughly democratic, more independent
of government and self-determining, and less
infested by parasitic classes, than perhaps any
in the world. There is no Priestly caste in China.
The only priests are Buddhist priests, who attend
to the little temples scattered here and there
on the wilder bits of land, among groves or rocks.
And they, in accordance with their religion, are
perfectly quiescent and unwilling to interfere with
the life of the people. There is, for the reasons
mentioned above, no Lawyer caste or profession.[2]
There is no Military caste. The profession of
arms, as already hinted, fell into contempt and

says : " There are four times as many judges in France
as in the whole Chinese Empire." And Simon (*La Cite
Chinoise*, p. 7) speaks strongly of the absence of crime.

[1] See Holcombe, *The Real Chinaman*, ch. ix.

[2] " The Chinese have an invincible repugnance to lawyers."
—*The Real Chinaman*, p. 30.

neglect a thousand years past, and until the date of the late Boxer movement there was no attempt to revive it. The Manchu dynasty, since its settlement in Peking, 250 years ago, has had a bodyguard of some 100,000 men permanently stationed in the neighborhood, but these soldiers, if soldiers they can be called, were till 1898 or so armed with bows and arrows, and were a mere rabble incapable of discipline or concerted action. The rest of the army in China consisted a few years ago of some 400,000 militia organised by the viceroys and governors of the different provinces, and constituting really fifteen different and independent armies, of which Chester Holcombe says that some were passably effective, while others he has seen were armed with old matchlocks and spears, and fans and umbrellas ! [1] It is evident from this that there has been till lately no military profession. China cannot even be said, as a whole, to have an army, for though the viceroys have each their bodies of militia, these act independently of one another.[2] And though doubtless, as I shall presently point out, there *will* be a united national

[1] *Chinese Question*, p. 129. See also account of a Chinese Military Review, by Mrs. A. Little, *Intimate China*, ch. xiv ; and Abbé Huc's *Chinese Empire*, vol. i, ch. x, on the absurdities of the Chinese Army. Now, however, all this is rapidly being altered.

[2] In the case of the Japano-Chinese War, for instance, the viceroys of the middle and south of China did not move at all, and sent no military help to Peking.

army, it will probably be a very long time, if ever, before the evils of militarism and the military caste grow up in this favored land.

That a country should exist in the world absolutely free from the dominance of the Priestly, the Legal, and the Military castes [1] seems to be too good to be true, and difficult indeed for the Western mind to believe ! But when we realise also that the Landlord living on rents and the Share or Bond holder living on the interest of capital lent out to others [2] are so rare as to be practically negligible—that there are, in fact, no landlord or capitalist *classes*— our wonder must surely deepen into admiration, possibly even to envy ; and we can hardly avoid asking ourselves the question whether what we have been pleased to call China's awakening may not, after all, mean the awakening of Europe !

However, do not let us go too fast. If in the socialist or semi-socialist nature of her institutions China is undoubtedly admirable, she equally certainly suffers from a defect which Socialism in Europe will have to be on its guard against, i.e. the bribery and corruption of officials, This

---

[1] And we may add the Medical profession ; see article on "Chinese Daily Life " by J. K. Goodrich, *Forum*, October 1899.

[2] " While in China comparatively few persons live in idleness on the income of their investments, an extraordinary number live on the profits of small capital which they administer themselves."—*Primitive Civilisations*, vol. ii, p. 330.

is the weak point of Chinese public life. The
' squeeze ' is universal.

The native residents of Peking have a saying, as describing
the universal peculation, that when the Imperial milk-wagon
reaches the outer gate of the city the official on duty there
takes out a cup of milk and puts in a cup of water. At each
gate and police-station within the city passed by the wagon
this process of extraction and substitution is repeated, with
the result that when the fluid eventually reaches the Imperial
table no trace of milk, even in color, can be detected. They
are also somewhat fond of saying that the Emperor is the
poorest man in all China.[1]

This illustration of the Imperial milk-wagon
apparently applies to the collection of taxes and
revenue all over the country. A tax is collected
by a minor official (often at considerably higher
than the legal rate), and is handed over to
superior officials, who in their turn deliver it
to the viceroy of the province. He finally has
to transfer it, or the balance of it, to the Imperial
Treasury. But the ' squeezes ' taken out at
each and every step of the process are so considerable and so numerous that the balance is
only small, and the Imperial Government remains
poor.

Chinese apologists for this state of affairs say
—and certainly with a good deal of truth—that
the salaries allowed to officials by Government
are merely nominal, and are recognised to be
so. The regular salary, for instance, of a viceroy
is only about £100 a year ; special allowances

[1] *The Real Chinese Question*, p. 357.

for this and that increase it to about £1,000 ; but of course the quite unavoidable expenses of the office far exceed the latter amount, and the public who pay the taxes are quite content that a portion of them should go to provide irregular additions to the regular allowance. So with other and lower officials. There is a good deal of give and take all through ; every family has relatives among the official classes, and these relatives in turn assist the family, so that the latter has an interest on both sides of the account, and if it is plundered it also shares in the plunder !—or, to put the matter less rudely, it permits and condones the ' squeeze ' as part of a system of necessary balances and adjustments.

So far the apologist ; and, as we have said, with some reason. Nevertheless we must feel that the system is a bad one, with all its irregularities and temptations to peculation, and not conducive to public morality. Especially in the towns and larger centres is this the case. In the country, probably, where everything has to be done more openly and publicly, the evils may be less.

What we have said about the smallness of the revenue flowing in to the Central Government and its small payments to officials—the " poverty of the Emperor " in fact—is important ; and there is no understanding of China without it. The Central Government is essentially feeble. It has little money ; it has no army ; it has next to

no police. What can it do? The people go
their own way. The taxes run to about 2s. 6d.
per head of the population.[1] Even if that were
all spent (say £50,000,000) on public purposes,
it would be a small amount for a nation of
400,000,000 population.[2] (What does our United
Kingdom, with a tenth of the population, spend?)
The Central Government is weak, and has no
power to coerce the people or compel them into
forms which they do not like. They go their
own way, rooted in the land and in the family,
and in their own customs.[3] Even the local
mandarins and officials—though sometimes doubtless they abuse their powers—are not by any
means independent of the people. Simon
describes a case in which a new mandarin

---

[1] *La Cité Chinoise*, p. 6. Compare also Sir Robert Hart in
"*These from the Land of Sinim*," p. 64 : "Government taxation
has always and everywhere been of the lightest possible
kind."

[2] Professor S. Wells Williams, reckoning the total revenue
(in 1883) at £40,000,000, estimates that of this only £11,000,000
would reach Peking, the rest being retained in the provinces.
—*The Middle Kingdom*, vol. i, p. 290.

[3] "The great fact to be noted, as between the Chinese and
their Government, is the almost unexampled liberty which
the people enjoy, and the infinitesimally small part which
Government plays in the scheme of national life."—*China in
Transformation*, by A. R. Colquhoun, p. 296.

"In point of fact the Chinese are governed less than any
nation in the world. . . . A thousand and one official in-
spections, interferences, and exactions, common everywhere
in America and Europe, are quite unknown in China."—*The
Real Chinese Question*, p. 4.

having been appointed, who was disliked by the
people, the people simply refused to have him,
and, politely but firmly turning his sedan-chair
round, sent him back to the place whence he
came.[1] And other instances of the same kind
are quoted. There is complete liberty of meeting and of the Press [2]—rights which are by no
means always accorded in Western countries—
and, as a matter of fact, discussion and the formation of public opinion are constantly going on
even in the smallest hamlets.

It is Western ignorance as to the real relation-
ship between the Central Government and the
people of China which is constantly leading even
our diplomatists (who ought to know better) into
all sorts of blunders. We make a treaty with
the Government at Peking (generally under threats
of force), and the Chinese Minister of course
smilingly defers and procrastinates, and finally
yields and signs the treaty. Yet he knows all
the time that it is waste paper. What power

[1] Simon puts the total number of officials for the whole of
China at under 30,000.—*La Cité Chinoise*, p. 15.
[2] Or there was till a few years ago. "To this day," says
Mrs. A. Little, "the Chinese peasant enjoys a degree of liberty
and immunity from Government interference unknown on
the Continent of Europe. There is no passport system; he
can travel where he pleases; he can form and join any kind
of association; his Press was free till the Empress Tze Hsi,
probably inspired by Russian influence, issued her edict
against it in 1898; his right of public meeting and free
speech are still unquestioned."—*Intimate China*, p. 378. See
also *La Cité Chinoise*, p. 17.

has he, or the Government, or the Emperor, to enforce the observation of the treaty by his own people? None at all. It may be a treaty to open up certain districts to our commercial agents, or for the remission of certain likin dues on foreign goods sent into the interior. Who can compel the people of that district to receive the hated foreigner, or who knows whether the local mandarins will remit those likin dues or not? [1] The Government can only send an order to the viceroy of each province ; the viceroy will use his own discretion ; he may pass the order on to the mandarins beneath him, or he may not. If he does they also will use their discretion ; finally the mandarins may bully the people, but the people, when all is said, will take their own ways, and on them will largely depend the final issue. China, in fact, is like an organism of the jelly-fish type, not very highly sensitive, not having any very marked and ruling centre to which everything is referred ; but for that very reason perhaps the more stable and persistent because its vitality is distributed throughout the whole mass.[2]

But the most interesting—and indeed astonish-

[1] See on this subject, *China in Transformation*, by A. R. Colquhoun, note, p. 163.
[2] A. R. Colquhoun very aptly compares China to a mass of protoplasm, and likens the family and village groups "to an infinite multitude of water-tight cells, which keep the whole mass afloat even in the most turbulent sea."—*China in Transformation*, p. 284.

ing—feature in the constitution of China is the
Han-Lin Academy and the influence it exercises.
In that country, where the military profession is
held in contempt and the merchant class accounted
lowest in public rank,[1] literature has for centuries
been held in the highest honor. Thousands of
candidates press to Peking and other cities every
year for the examinations. To take the degrees,
to become a member of the privileged and
literary class, respected everywhere, and so to
have a chance of gaining official position, is the
aim of millions. The poorest families will make
heroic sacrifices to enable one of their members
to become a scholar. It is said that there must
be some 700,000 Chinese graduates now living.
So widespread indeed is the interest in literature
that it is quite common to find holiday-folk (as
is seen also in Japan) spending their afternoon
in the country capping verses or writing odes in
amicable rivalry.

The Han-lin College or Academy was founded
in A.D. 740,[2] or nearly 1,200 years ago, by an
Emperor of the Han dynasty, as a sort of advisory
body. It now consists of some 240 members,
each of whom is granted by the State a house

[1] The four grades of the Chinese polity, in order of respect,
are said to be *shih, nung, kung,* and *shang,* or scholar, farmer,
artisan, and merchant. The first are the brains, the second
the producers, the third the producers at second-hand, and
the fourth the mere exchangers.

[2] The literary class and examination system, however, had
existed long before this.

and garden and a modest pecuniary allowance. But it has these privileges as an immemorial right, and is in no way dependent on the Government ; on the contrary, it has the right, and it is part of its duty, to criticise the latter, and even the Emperor himself. The College *elects itself* —that is, when a vacancy occurs it elects the new member, and of course always from those who are already most distinguished as scholars. Thus, like our Fellows' bodies and learned societies in the West, it keeps up its own traditions. Its duties are (1) discussion, (2) dissemination of its conclusions throughout the nation, and (3) censorship of individuals (officials).

It discusses anything : any question which affects the welfare of the people. This may be a foreign treaty, or it may be a new method in education, or it may be some small detail in agriculture. *But the College has no legislative or executive power*. It can neither pass a law nor issue a command of any kind. All it can do is, when it has arrived at a conclusion, to issue a leaflet or pamphlet on the subject. This may be a leaflet recommending some method of dealing with an insect pest in the gardens, it may be a pamphlet protesting against a foreign treaty, or it may (as happened lately) be one urging the adoption of Western science in the schools. Whatever it is, the circular has an enormous publicity ; it goes by millions of copies through the land, and is read and debated in every little hamlet. And If the recommendations suggested meet with a wide and warm public approval it not infrequently happens that the Government takes them up, and they pass into the laws or institutions of the country. Very little, I believe, ever passes into the public law in China without this previous circulation and approving discussion—for the simple reason that without this there would be no security that the people would conform to it.

II

I have dwelt thus long upon the conditions of life in China without coming to the gist of my paper, namely the results which may be expected from the contact of that life with Western civilisation—because, in fact, without a fair understanding of the former it is impossible to estimate the latter.

The first awakening of China to the growth of what we call the modern Western world undoubtedly occurred in 1839–40, when the guns of British frigates at Canton boomed out our demand for the admission of opium into that port. Into the details of that oft-told tale, so dishonoring to Britain, it is not necessary for us to go. China for centuries had taken her own way in complete ignorance and indeed oblivion of the outer world. Now suddenly the whole proceedings opened her eyes to two great facts :

(1) The existence of nations there in the " West " possessed of demonic powers and hellish engines of destruction ; (2) their apparently entire unscrupulousness in the use of these powers in the service of gain and trading profit. Considering that the trader, as we have already pointed out, ranks as the lowest class in the Chinese polity, and that trade (as apart from industrial *production*) has always been looked upon as beneath the notice of the ruling classes and officials—that it is, in fact, almost impossible to get them to take any interest in it—one can begin to understand the strange and sinister impression produced. Naturally it was many years before the new tidings about the " barbarians " and " foreign devils " penetrated the whole mass of the nation. But unfortunately succeeding events did nothing to remove the first impression, only confirmed it. Envoys from Britain, France, and the United States pressed for right of residence in China, always in the name of Trade, and backed their demands always by Force. China persistently refused their admittance, but in 1860 a combined force of English and French destroyed the Taku forts,[1] captured Tientsin, and the Peking Legations were established. Other events of the same character followed, and with the same result. The Chinese, overwhelmed by force, had to give

[1] On the plea that the Chinese had not observed the treaty of 1858; but we have already seen what the nature of a Chinese treaty must be.

way. Always the Western war vessels grew larger and more threatening, always their cannon more terrible and destructive. Till in 1894-5 came the Japan and China war, and, with the defeat of China, loud and open talk among the Western Powers of her dismemberment.

It was only then, just at the close of the last century, and after some fifty or sixty years of rude awakening cuffs and blows, that China *en masse* began to rouse herself to meet the situation. Her haughty and ignorant contempt of the Western peoples as mere hordes of savages [1] was giving way to astonishment at their mechanical and scientific powers, if also with added hatred of them because of their powers. Japan had already tackled the problem, had educated and armed herself, but China lay helpless and incapable. What was to be done? A huge popular movement—the ' Boxer ' movement—ignorant and superstitious, but full of enthusiasm and determination to oust the foreigner, began to grow up. And the Han-Lin Academy came in to make appeal to the more thoughtful part of the nation.

The action of the Academy in this matter is full of interest and suggestion, and I must dwell on it for a moment. As a rule it would appear that the Academy is a somewhat conservative

[1] Even as late as 1864 the Chinese Government "declined to negotiate a treaty with the Kingdom of Prussia, because it had never heard of any such country !"—*The Real Chinese Question*, p. 185.

body, bound up, no doubt, to a great extent with
the old national ideals and the Confucian tradition ; but, having debated this matter of the
foreigner, it seems that a majority was in favor
of issuing an appeal to the country—a call to
arms, in fact, and a call to Western science and
education. The writing of this appeal was com-
mitted to Chang Chih Tung, China's "greatest
viceroy," and the pamphlet, presented by the
Academy and endorsed by the Emperor, was duly
printed and circulated. It has probably by now
circulated by millions of copies.[1]   China's only
hope, the author explains, consists in the
strengthening of her army and military power
by the adoption of modern methods and imple-
ments of war ; in the improvement of her schools
by the introduction of science and Western teaching ; and in getting into touch with Western
ideas by means of travel, translation of books,
etc.   At the same time the solid and world-old
bases of Chinese life and citizenship, the laws
of Confucius, and the worship of the ancestors,
must by no means be deserted, for it is only
on these that a secure edifice can be erected.

The following are some quotations from the
book. Speaking of education in the schools, the
author says (page 100) :—

---

[1] A translation of this pamphlet, called *China's Only Hope*
(Oliphant, Anderson, & Ferrier, 1901), pp. 150, can now be
obtained, and is well worth reading. Its circulation in China,
prior to translation in 1900, was put at a million copies.

The old and new must both be taught ; by the old is meant the Four Books, the Five Classics, history, government, and geography of China ; by the new, *Western* government, science, and history. Both are imperative, but we repeat that the old is to form the basis, and the new is for practical purposes. Under the head of Western Government come the comparative study of governments and science, colleges, geography, political economy, customs, taxes, military regula- tions, laws, and expositions. Under Western science are classed mathematics, mining, therapeutics, sound, light, chemistry, and electricity.

Among other suggestions for providing money for these improved schools, he says —

Convert the temples and monasteries of the Buddhists and Taoists into schools.[1] To-day these exist in myriads. Every important city has more than a hundred. Temple lands and incomes are in most cases attached to them. If all these are appropriated to educational purposes we guarantee plenty of money and means to carry out the plan (p. 99).

We must put the useful books of the West into Chinese, and scatter them far and wide among those who are ignorant of Western languages, among the wide-awake officials, the impecunious *literati*, the scholars replete with Confucian lore, the merchants, workmen, the old and the young, to be used and appropriated by them in their different spheres (p. 113).

Travel must not be neglected.

The diminutive country of Japan has suddenly sprung into prominence. Ito, Yamagata, Yanomoto, Mitsui, and others

[1] This advice was actually followed to some extent ; but after the seizure of the throne by the Dowager Empress the temples and monasteries were restored to their former uses. (See *The Story of China*, by R. K. Douglas, p. 454.) In the last few years, however, some fifteen new universities have been established.

visited foreign countries twenty years ago, and learned a method by which to escape the coercion of Europe. Under their leadership more than one hundred Japanese students were sent to Germany, France, and England to learn foreign systems of conducting government, commerce, war, etc. After these had completed their course they were recalled and employed by the Japanese Government as generals and Ministers. When the Government was once changed they developed into the Heroes of the Orient (p. 92).

And he goes on to urge the sending of Chinese students to Japan and the West, for a similar purpose. Railways must also be constructed.

Let us build railways, and then the scholars can have easy communication with distant friends, the farmer can utilise much that is now waste, the merchant can readily meet the demand for supply, forwarding the heaviest material, the workmen will soon find machinery everywhere, the abundant products of the mines will be beneficially distributed, and our China coast will be securely protected and guarded by myriads of efficient troops. . . . The whole country will become really ours, and China will be one great united family, with no fear of famine or war (p. 126).

As to the nations of Europe, there is no trust to be placed in their promises ; they are

like tigers with dripping jaws (p. 81). They talk of peace and mean war. Austria first instituted the Disarmament Society. Immediately afterwards the war between Russia and Turkey broke out. Then Germany attacked Africa, England attacked Egypt and Thibet, France conquered Madagascar, and Spain Cuba. . . . Germany has seized upon our Kiaochou, and Russia has appropriated our Port Arthur. . . . If we talk of disarmament to the other countries without the force to back up our words we will become the laughing-stock of the world. . . . *Drilling* troops is better than disbanding them. With fifty warships on the sea and thirty myriads of troops on land,

with daily additions to both ships and troops, with the daily
strengthening of our forts and equipping them with the best
engines of modern warfare, and with the railways intersecting
the land, what country would dare to begin hostilities with
China or in any way infringe upon her treaty rights? Under
these conditions Japan will side with China, Europe will retire,
and the Far East will be at rest (p. 140).

Finally, comparing China with the West, he
says :—

~ Although China is not so wealthy and powerful as the West,
her people of whatever condition—rich or poor, high or low—
all enjoy a perfect freedom and a happy life. Not so all the
inhabitants of Western lands. Their Governments may be
strong; but the lower classes of the people are miserable,
unhappy, and maliciously wronged. Their liberties are re-
strained, and there is no redress. They rise in rebellion on
every opportunity, and not a year passes without an account
of the murder of some King or the stabbing of some Minister.
These Governments certainly cannot be compared with our
China (p. 41).

I have given these copious extracts from the
book because I think they are surely very interesting—not only as giving the words of a great
Chinese statesman, but as representing the views
of, at any rate, a large section of the Han-Lin
Academy, and a *résumé* of the program which
is now, one may say without exaggeration, being
discussed by peasant and prince alike all over
the vast demesne of Chinese territory.

This program is in fact—though of course
there are dissentients to it—being rapidly carried
out. We know what Japan has done ; but China
is far older and more experienced than Japan.

If on the one hand she is more wary and slow to move, she is, on the other, equally capable, and, when she moves, inclined to move more permanently and more irresistibly than the younger nation. The Boxer uprising was, and is, largely [1] the instinctive solution of the problem by the popular masses. It put power into the hands of the Empress Dowager for her *coup d'état*, and she and her party in turn supported and reinforced it. It led to the attacks on the Peking Legations in 1900. It meant, and means, " Out with the foreigner " and " China for the Chinese." And the movement has come to stay. Sir Robert Hart, who probably knew China as well as any living Englishman, said : " In fifty years' time there will be millions of Boxers in serried ranks and war's panoply at the call of the Chinese Government ; there is not the slightest doubt of that." [2] Nor can we for a moment doubt that the Chinese, though averse to change, have just as great technical ability as the Japanese, and if they once come to realise the need of its application in modern arts of war or peace will excel, just as the Japanese have done. The telegraph and telephone, at their first appearance, were resisted to the utmost ; but now already their wires reach like a web all over the Flowery Land. The people are like

[1] Though it seems also that it was greatly stimulated by the publication of *China's Only Hope* (see p. 6 of that book).
[2] " *These from the Land of Sinim*," p. 55.

that—tenacious of old custom, yet once in motion exceedingly quick to take up a new position. And Sir Robert Hart warmly endorses the words of Wên Hsiang, the Prime Minister of China in the early sixties, who said ꜱ—

You are all too anxious to awake us and start us on a new road, and you will do it ; but you will all regret it, for, once awake and started, we shall go fast and far—farther than you think—much farther than you want ! [1]

To this movement of China against the foreigner and towards her own independence the victory of Japan over Russia gave something like a seal of security. The autonomy of the Far East is now established, and China has only to follow the lead of Japan in cultivation of the arts of war, and the two in combination may set the world at defiance. Already for some years Chinese emissaries and inspectors have been keeping their eyes open in our big steel workshops. Indeed as far back as 1872 the Viceroy Li Hung Chang sent 120 Chinese boys of good family to be educated in the United States, with a view to studying military and naval methods there. Now there are some thousands of young Chinese studying military science either in China or Japan. There are nineteen modern military academies in China, three arsenals turning out rifles and quick-firing guns, and more in process of forma-

[1] " These from the Land of Sinim," p. 52.

tion.[1] Very soon, says Putnam Weale, they will have a thoroughly effective army of some 400,000 men, all trained on the Japanese system. Needless to say the European Powers and the United States have learned a lesson, and all talk of dismemberment has ceased.

We may take it, I think, as good as certain that China will rehabilitate her military power, and that (even though there may be attempts against her) there will be no dismemberment. There remain other questions. What about the "Yellow Peril" of invasion?—400,000,000 of Chinese let loose upon the world! What about the awakening of China to trade and commercial life, and the result upon our trades? What about the infiltration of Chinese ideas and social standards among the Western peoples?

1. I think that whoever has followed the general outline of Chinese life and character will find it very difficult to imagine this people deliberately making an armed invasion of other countries. The whole tenor of their temperament and institutions is "Let alone!" "Don't meddle!" They have no dogmatic religion (a frequent cause of wars) to carry at the point of the sword into other countries. They have no strong central government (another frequent cause) ready to serve private ends by the wholesale sacrifice of

[1] *The Re-shaping of the Far East*, by Putnam Weale (1905), vol. ii, ch. xxxiii.

its own subjects. Their ancestral worship pre-
cludes them from forming permanent homes in
other lands. In all the long history of the
Chinese Empire there is, I believe, hardly a
single instance of their invading, in a military
sense, another country.[1] The habits of the
people are agricultural and social—not military ;
the Government, as I have said, is weak and
diffused, and though the latter may, in the face
of foreign menaces, pull itself together (and is
doing so) sufficiently to present a good front
against invasion, it seems very improbable that
it will ever concentrate to the much greater
degree necessary for the invasion of other lands.
On the other hand, the eternal problem of Chinese
life—namely the sustenance of so enormous a
population on an area of land which, though
large, is limited—may one day reach a point of
acuteness compelling some kind of irruption
beyond their borders. In that case—though it
be rash to prophesy—I should think a huge (but
peaceful) migration is the most likely thing to
happen. And if the infiltration of Western ideas
were to go so far (which does not at present
seem probable) as to break up the Chinaman's
conception of the sanctity of home, and to deaden
his urgent desire for burial in ancestral ground
—then indeed such migrations might assume pro-
portions quite alarming, and even threatening to

[1] The invasions of Japan and Burmah under Kublai Khan
cannot fairly be credited to the Chinese.

the stability of our own civilisations.[1] However, I think we may put migrations of this magnitude off to a rather remote period, and say for the present that while there is going to be no dismemberment of China by the Western or other Powers, there is, on the other hand, going to be no "Yellow Peril" in the shape of armed invasions of these lands by China.[2]

2. The question of the commercial relations of the New China with Europe and the West is a very interesting one. I think myself that,

[1] Professor Douglas points out (*Story of China*, p. 2) that throughout their history the Chinese have mainly conquered other lands by the process of *settling* on them !

[2] Unfortunately the same cannot be said with regard to the Japanese. The lust of invasion or conquest seems to be attracting them; there is much in the character and religion of the people antagonistic to it. Anyhow the possibility of the overthrow of our Western civilisation by peaceful migrations from the East must not be ignored. To quote Lafcadio Hearn (*Out of the East*, pp. 237–41) :— "Already thinkers, summarising the experience of the two colonising nations—thinkers not to be ignored, both French and English—have predicted that the earth will never be fully dominated by the races of the West, and that the future belongs to the Orient. . . . In the simple power of living our so-called higher races are immensely inferior to the races of the Far East. . . . For the Oriental has proved his ability to study and to master the results of our science upon a diet of rice, and on so simple a diet can learn to manufacture and to utilise our most complicated inventions. But the Occidental cannot live except at a cost sufficient for the maintenance of twenty Oriental lives. In our very superiority lies the secret of our fatal weakness. Our physical machinery requires a fuel too costly to pay for the running of it in a perfectly conceivable future period of race-competition and pressure of population."

though there is a large party in China in favor of the "ring-fence" policy, the "open-door" party, supported by Chang Chih Tung, and reinforced by the general tendency of trade development, etc., will almost inevitably gain ground. The more obvious advantages of this policy, the influx of cheap goods, etc., will appeal after a time to the masses of the people ; and once the nation, by the establishment of its military strength, has come to feel itself secure, it may possibly be considerably more disposed to admit the trader and the commercial traveler than it has hitherto been. Having mounted its guns, it will not be so afraid of opening the door.

If we suppose the door opened, and (what is already part accomplished) a network of railways giving access to the interior of China, then —for good or evil, and let us hope, for good— a big trade with the Western nations must inevitably spring up. There will, for many years and until the people can manufacture these things for themselves, be a great demand for our steel rails, girders, edge tools, machines, etc., as well as for some classes of our textile fabrics ; [1] and we in return shall be buying Chinese silks, tea, porcelain, spices, etc., more freely. Both parties will no doubt so far be benefited. Then a time will come when, for good or evil, our manufactures and methods of manufacture, our factory

[1] The increase in the export of Manchester cotton goods to China has been enormous during the last few years.

system in short, will make headway in China—
when they will produce steel rails, big guns, and
calico sheeting for themselves ; and their workers,
as wage-workers, will begin to be crowded by
thousands in huge workshops to the sound of
machinery.[1]

What will happen then? It is hard to say.
Already in Japan, in a few short years, the introduction of Western commercialism has brought
with it problems unknown before—dire increase
of poverty, multiplication of unemployed.[2] What
will it do in China? There already the supply
of labor is so great that the land is like a cup
full to the very brim. Introduce labor-saving
machinery, and instantly it will overflow. Millions
will be thrown out of work. Terrible commotion
and uproar will ensue. Will China plod through
all this, through a long period of bloodshed and
confusion, to land herself at last only where the
Western nations have landed themselves, in the
production of a futile society composed of two
great classes antagonistic to each other, and both

---

[1] It must be remembered that China is well supplied with
coal. "Coal exists in every province," says Wells Williams
in *The Middle Kingdom*. The whole of Southern Shansi is
full of coal—beds five, eight, and even ten feet thick. The
world could, according to Richtofen, be supplied with coal
from Shansi alone for thousands of years ! Coal and iron are
also abundant in Yunnan. Cotton mills and ironworks already
exist in Hanyang, Shanghai, and other places.—See *China in
Transformation*, by A. R. Colquhoun, ch. iii and ch. v.
[2] See Lafçadio Hearn, *Japan, an Interpretation.*

unsatisfactory—one living idly on dividends and the other in a state of monotonous and squalid slavery? It is hardly thinkable. Or will her genius, already so deeply Socialistic, seize on and transform this factory system into a free organisation of guilds,[1] self-dependent and autonomous, sweated by no masters, and ready to use the surplus productiveness of machinery for the shortening of the hours of labor and the absorption of unemployed into the working ranks? We cannot tell. The world can only at present wait, in profound suspense and interest, to see what solution will be given.

That a considerable and important movement in China is imminent seems at least very probable ; and this may lead, at any rate for a time, to a great influx of Chinese into Western countries, and to some amount of dislocation of Western trade. With regard to the latter, the production on a large scale of factory-made goods in China and at a very low cost has been held up by not a few writers[2] as heralding a period of great disaster to the Western nations ; but we think this view is based on a misconception.

[1] The Chinese guilds and mutual help societies are most numerous—clubs of young men for starting each other in business; clubs for insurance, burial, recreation, etc. ; masonic clubs ; secret societies for political purposes, and so forth. "The Chinese have a genius for association," says A. R. Colquhoun, *China in Transformation*, p. 297.

[2] See Professor C. H. Pearson in *National Life and Character*, p. 133 ; also E. Simon in *La Cité Chinoise*, p. 85.

The entry of China into the world-market, with cheap goods in her hands, would undoubtedly alter the *currents* of Western trade, causing some items to increase and others to diminish in magnitude. An offer from her, for instance, of good and inexpensive cotton cloths to the world would strike a heavy blow at Lancashire. But —since exports always demand imports in return— if China came into the world-market as a seller, she would also come to the same extent as a *buyer*. The total volume of Western trade would not be diminished, rather increased. Even if Britain lost in one branch of her trade she would probably be the gainer in another The new arrival would mean a temporary dislocation of Western trade, but it would by no means spell disaster.

There are some also who think that with the development of self-supply through machine and factory production, combined with her own enormous natural internal resources, China will be tempted to abate and ultimately to drop her trade with the West, and to retire once more within her ring-fence. But again—though prophecy is rash—I do not think such a retirement is likely. There is much current misunderstanding of the laws of foreign trade, and the subject is a difficult one, without doubt ; but this much is certain, that—granted Free Trade and no artificial walls of Protection around a country—that country, even though capable of producing *everything* it needs

within its own borders, will still prefer to exchange some of its products with other countries ;
and that the more flourishing it is within its own
borders the more active probably will its outer
exchange be.

It is often thought that if the cost of production of a certain article is higher, say, in Britain
than in some other country, there is no chance
of that article being demanded from Britain by
the said country. But J. S. Mill has conclusively
proved that this is not so (*Principles of Political
Economy*, Book III, ch. xvii). To use his classic
example, if the cost of production of both cloth
and corn is greater in Britain than in Poland,
it may still happen that British cloth will flow
steadily to Poland, and Polish corn flow steadily
to Britain, simply because cloth is cheaper *relatively* to corn in Britain, and corn cheaper
relatively to cloth in Poland.[1]

If China, conscious of her own strength, should
cast off her prejudice against mercantile relations with the outer world, there is little doubt
that she will always find advantage to herself
in such relations—both buying and selling. And
if the Western nations desire to make her their
customer, it seems to me that there is probably

---

[1] And so a certain amount of corn sent from Poland would
buy more cloth in Britain at British prices than the same
amount of corn remaining in Poland would buy of Polish
cloth at Polish prices. But the whole chapter should be
referred to. See pp. 222, 223 *infra*.

no better way to do so than to acknowledge her
autonomy, give her every pledge of security, and
favor in all ways her internal prosperity—and
so leave the natural laws of trade and exchange
to work themselves out.   Lord Salisbury, in a
moment of inspiration, once said—

> If I am asked what our policy in China is, my answer is
> very simple. It is to maintain the Chinese Empire, to pre-
> vent it from falling into ruins, to invite it into paths of
> reform, and to give it every assistance which we are able to
> give it to perfect its defence or to increase its commercial
> prosperity.[1]

And surely, a wise and generous national policy
in the future *will* recognise this great principle
in all foreign trade, that the prosperity of the
peoples we deal with also spells our own
prosperity.

3. We now come to the third and final
question, namely the effect of China's awakening
in the way of the interchange of ideas between
her and the West.   This contact between West
and East is one of the most remarkable characteristics of the present age, and one surely fraught
with great and important issues for the future.
On all sides we see both Eastern and Western
peoples being modified by it.   The commercial
system is breaking down caste in India.   The
interest in modern science there is growing.
Huxley and Darwin seem for the moment to

[1] See Mrs. Archibald Little's *Intimate China*, p. 424.

be taking the place of the Vedic sages. On the other hand, in Europe our philosophy is being profoundly altered by Eastern thought, and among the peoples at home doctrines of Karma and Reincarnation are being widely (and even wildly) circulated. Japan has adopted battleships, tall chimneys, and chimney-pot hats ; and we āre making a pious cult of Japanese art and Japanese simplicity of life. How far is this going to go? Are Asia and Europe going to blend in a uniform color of civilisation, all alike for the whole globe? and is humanity entering on a last stage of universal Esperanto and Equality? To suppose this would, I think, be a little too previous. While it is perfectly true that India and Japan are being greatly modified by contact with the West, and that the Western nations āre being largely colored by Eastern thought and custom—and greatly to the benefit of both—it is also true that, looking deeper, there is no sign of a radical change of base. India, in view of com- mercialism, may sweep away many absurdities of her present caste system, but there is no sign that she will abandon its great main outlines, which she has preserved inviolate for thirty centuries. Something the same with her religious philosophy. She will correct that to the data of modern science, but she will not desert it. And so with Japan. While it was thought a little time ago that Japan was becoming completely transmogrified in her blind devotion to Western ways and manners, it has now become clear that her full and conscious intention is in a very different direction—namely, merely to adapt and make use of these Western things for the better protection and ultimate expression of her own ideals. She is returning to her own base again instead of going farther from it. As Lafcadio Hearn says (*Out of the East*, ch. vii, " Jiujutsu ") :—

Despite her railroad and steamship lines, her telegraphs and telephones, her postal service and her express companies, her steel artillery and magazine rifles, her universities and technical schools, she remains just as Oriental to-day as she was a thousand years ago. She has been able to remain herself, and to profit to the utmost possible limit by the strength of the enemy. She has been, and still is, defending herself by the most admirable system of intellectual defence ever heard of—by a marvelous national jiujutsu.

We may apply these remarks to China. The vast probabilities are that China, adopting like Japan a great deal of Western civilisation and thought, will still not move perceptibly from her ancient base of 4,000 years. And when we consider how excellent that base is—fixed deep in the Land, in the Family, in the great moral principles of good Citizenship, and in a Religion spiritual yet void of all dogma—there seems indeed no reason why she should leave it. That the challenge and intrusion of the Western world will benefit China one can hardly doubt. Wrapped and isolated in her own life for centuries, she has certainly lapsed into much feebleness, ignorance, and mere stupid routine ; but the sleeper is very far from dead or disabled. Awaking from her dreams she may any day now astonish the world by activities as remarkable as those of Japan, though probably along a different line ; and she may, with her long past of experience, leap to the solution of social problems which are almost the despair of the West.

In the West itself the growing knowledge of China, and familiarity with her institutions, hitherto so little understood, will surely have a profound influence—a greater influence than that exercised by Japan. About the Japanese civilisation there is a certain lightness of touch, almost a thinness ; but China is massive and solid to a degree. When it comes to be recognised what are the causes of China's immense duration down the centuries—the democratic simplicity of her institutions, her affection for the land and determination that every one shall have a share in it, her freedom from parasite classes, and her recognition of the farmer and the artisan as superior to the merchant in importance ; the respect, too, paid to letters, to the clan and to the family, the easy handling of domestic, social, and legal matters through these powers, the little power of central government, the genius of the people for the formation of free guilds and societies, and so on—it is not

difficult to see that the European peoples will
be inclined to rub their eyes and take many a
hint from those they have hitherto despised.
Again it is rash to prophesy—but it may be
that the fact of the Awakening of the East
coming now, at a time when Europe (as we
hope) is growing out of her commercial *regime*
into nobler ideals, may make a *rapprochement*
between East and West all the easier. It has
been the fatal and vulgar commercialism of the
Westerners which has for long been the greatest
barrier between us and the East. "The entire
Western atmosphere," says Chester Holbrook, " is
intensely repugnant to the Chinese. They have
never understood nor admitted that the main
purpose for which governments were created was
to foster commerce and money-making. From
their view-point that is the petty business of petty
men." When this obstacle on our side is partly
removed there will be the less temptation to China
to retire behind her own walls. The peaceful
infiltration, too, of Chinese folk into Western lands
—which, apart from any more serious movement,
will surely go on—and of Chinese of better class
(not as hitherto the mere riff-raff and family
outcasts), will lead in the same direction and to
a better understanding ; and may contribute to
that great change which one day perhaps will
be called the Awakening of the West.

APPENDIX

THE UNEMPLOYED RICH AND THE UN-
EMPLOYED POOR

(See ch. ii, p. 9.)

A MOMENT'S thought shows that as machinery perfects and perfects itself there is a tendency for fewer workers to produce more goods or wealth. The balance of increased wealth goes to the profit-receiving classes ; and so there is a double result, namely, the increase of the wealthy unemployed, and the increase of the unemployed workers. The increase of these two classes may not go on simultaneously, and there may and must be fluctuations on both sides ; but the general tendency is clear. It might, of course, be counteracted by shorter hours of labor and increased wage, which by bringing a greater number of workers in under better conditions would immensely improve their lot, and at the same time by reducing profits would clean up and improve the lives of the wealthy ; but as the entire tendency of the present system is the other way (in order to keep *up* profits), this double shrinkage of employment must go on—as long, in fact, as the system goes on, and until the whole attitude of the nation towards these questions changes.

THE MINIMUM WAGE

*A Paper read at the Conference on Sweated Industries,
at Glasgow, October 12, 1907.*

(See ch. ii, p. 14.)

THE subject of the Minimum Wage has been very
widely considered in various aspects and from various
points of view ; and I do not propose now to go into
the general question. There is evidently a growing
public opinion in favor of the constitution of Wages
Boards and the establishment of some kind of legal
minimum ; and doubtless something will be done in
that direction. There will be difficulties, of course, in
drafting regulations, and there will be drawbacks to
their operation, but these are things we must expect
in any such case. I am now only desirous to establish a point which has, I think, not been sufficiently
insisted on ; and which will, I hope, remove one class
of prejudice against, or objection to, the proposal.

It is generally tacitly assumed that a legal Minimum,
by raising wages in low classes of labor, will handicap the employer, make the realising of a profit more
difficult, and generally place a strain upon him, which
latter, of course, he may overcome, but which will
nevertheless remain a strain. I want to point out that
in many respects this is the reverse of what will
happen. And I believe that quite a few employers
are beginning to realise that this is so, and therefore

are favorable to a legal enactment—though no doubt the majority still are opposed to it.

The case in reality is very simple. Every one knows that the employer to-day has a most anxious time. The dread of competition, the continual fluctuations of prices, the fear of being undersold in the market, haunt him. He has no certain foundation for his business. He is like a man standing or working on boggy ground, with no firm footing anywhere. At any moment a competitor may undersell him ; and one of the commonest causes of such underselling is the employment of cheap labor. Here are three manufacturers, say, in some particular branch of industry, all fairly equal with one another, and all going along fairly well. Then, all at once, a fourth comes in, with sweated labor, undersells the others, and breaks up the trade. Painful fluctuations and disturbances set in, prices come down, ruinous alike to employers and employed ; and ultimately perhaps the former, even against their own wish, are forced to adopt the wage-cutting devices of their new competitor.

Now we must contend that to rule out or prevent this operation by fixing a minimum below which the wage shall *not* go, is a benefit, not only to the employed, but to the employers themselves. It gives them at last some firm ground beneath their feet. It takes away one large cause of doubt and risk and uncertainty ; and simplifies greatly for them the problem which they are handling.

Imagine ten or twelve men—a sight you may often see in large ironworks—standing round in a circle and holding a heavy iron plate, which they have to handle and perhaps pass on to some machine ; and imagine the ground on which those men stand to be partly big boulders and partly mud. You will appreciate at once the dangers and difficulty of their work. At one moment the plate will be tilted in this direction, throwing an unbearable weight on one man ; at another moment it will be tilted in that. No man will have certain footing or be able to use his strength properly. Now suppose them all to step up 6 inches onto a solid and level stone pavement. It may be a slight exertion to get there, but once there, the whole conditions will be different. The work will be carried on with a certainty, an ease, and an economy of labor, out of all comparison with what existed before. Somewhat corresponding will be the advantages to employers when by the fixation of a minimum wage the financial ground beneath their feet shall have been made comparatively solid, and the conditions so far equal for all.

Trade Unions, of course, have already done something of the kind in the higher grades of industry ; and I believe that many employers are quite ready to admit that their action has been helpful. The Unions have, in fact, secured their trades to some degree against ruinous fluctuations. It is only necessary to imagine for a moment the effect of the total disappearance of the Unions—say in the Lancashire Cotton trade—to realise that such a disappearance would mean widespread confusion—the pushing in of new competitors with cheap or sweated labor, the bankruptcy of old employers, and endless disturbance and chaos in a great industry.

The truth is that, within limits, it does not matter to an Employer if wages *are* high, provided all other employers have to pay equally high. It may matter to the *Public*, of course (who may have to pay a higher price for the article), but not to the Employer. We come, therefore, now to the question of the interest of the Public.

That the absence of a Minimum Wage (whether that minimum be obtained by Trade Unions or by Wages Boards) may mean a cheapening of price to the public, must of course be admitted. But, at this time of day, I think no one will say that that *in itself* constitutes a sufficient reason. We all feel that any such gain to the Public might be very ill secured by the degradation and misery of a large body of workers. And in the case of the so-called Sweated Industries—with which we are specially dealing—there are reasons for supposing that the enhancement in price (due to the minimum regulation) would be almost imperceptible. In these industries wages often bear such a very small ratio to cost of materials, profits, salaries of superintendence, etc., that a rise of wages need make but little difference in the price of the article.

Take the case of shirts that are "made"[1] at from 8d. to 1s. a dozen—say, one shirt made for 1d. That shirt is sold for 2s. Doubtless in some cases for more. Suppose the woman's wage *doubled*, so that she will get 2d. instead of 1d. Her week's wage will in consequence rise from, say, 7s. to 14s.—which latter, though a poor enough wage, will be positive affluence to her. The price of the shirt, other things remaining the same, will rise 1d. The shirt, therefore, would cost 2s. 1d. instead of 2s. Can we suppose that it would be hard on the public to ask them to pay 2s. 1d. for the shirt, in order that a whole class of miserable workers should be redeemed to better conditions?—or can we suppose that the demand for shirts would be diminished by this extra charge? The more probable result of it all, of course, would be that the 2s.

[1] The term "making" does not include cutting out, sewing on buttons, and making buttonholes, but it includes practically everything else.

price would remain as before, and that the employer would accept a slightly reduced profit.

Nor must we forget a thing which is constantly being overlooked when these questions of better wages are being discussed, namely, that markets, instead of being ruined by better wages, are greatly stimulated thereby—for to-day Political Economy is beginning to see, much more clearly than of old, that markets and trade rest on the well-being of the mass of the peoples—that is, on the mass-wages. Whatever, therefore, cripples wages and the welfare of the masses necessarily cripples trade and the markets. Into such a general question of Political Economy, however—interesting as it might be to discuss—we must not go now.

I would say a word on the difficult subject of Foreign Trade—because it almost necessarily links up with the question we have in hand.

My argument has run upon the assumption that a Minimum Wage, though it might raise the cost of production of an article to some degree, need in nowise handicap an employer, because it would apply to all employers alike. And this argument I consider perfectly just, as long as it is applied, say, within the limits of the United Kingdom. But we have to consider besides (what is undoubtedly a fact) that trade runs nowadays on such small margins that a slight enhancement of the cost of production may—I do not say necessarily will, but *may*—drive an industry abroad.

There are two points I should like to bring forward in this connexion : (1) That the difficulty will have to be. met, and is being met, by the extension of the principle of the Minimum Wage to other countries ; (2) that in general, the bogey of Foreign Competition —though not without a certain basis of reality—has been made far too much of, and has become a cause of alarm far greater than there is any reason for.

With regard to (1), we know that Australia and New Zealand have for some time had Wages Boards and Arbitration Courts in operation (Sir C. Dilke's Bill was founded on the Victorian Wages Boards), while America has had a system of licensing home-work-rooms. Germany, our chief rival in the sweated trades, is strong against Sweating, and an Imperial Commission is considering now the question of steps to be taken. So that these facts should rather encourage us in the direction we are going, and towards the establishment of an International Agreement on the subject.

With regard to (2), namely, Foreign Trade, there is no doubt a great deal of nonsense talked on the subject. I fear folk nowadays do not read their John Stuart Mill as they ought to ! Of course, it would be absurd to deny that sometimes a rise in the cost of production at home may cause a foreign demand to cease ; but this is by no means always the case, [and (paradoxical as it may sound) it may often happen that a foreign country may demand from us an article which it is actually producing all the time at less cost than we are at home.

Trade, in fact, does not follow absolute cheapness, but relative cheapness. It may happen that a thing (a razor, say) is produced cheaper in Germany than here, and yet the Germans may continue buying it from us because *relatively* to some article the Germans export to us that razor is cheaper here than in Germany. Germany sends butter to Britain because, relatively to certain other things, it is of more value here than in Germany. A keg of butter, say, will buy twenty razors here, but only fifteen of the same class in Germany. It will pay a German merchant, therefore, to send butter to England, and take our razors in exchange—and a steady interchange of butter and razors will go on—even though the cost of razors in both countries is the same, say 1s. each. That is, we shall export razors to Germany, even though they are produced equally cheaply there as here. Now, suppose the cost of razors in Britain to rise a little, so as to be actually greater than in Germany—say, only nineteen can be obtained for a keg of butter instead of twenty. Still the exchange will go on, because there will still be a gain of four razors on each keg. (I am, of course, not mentioning costs of transit, etc., because those things, though they will alter the figures, will not alter the general principle.) In this case, then, we shall actually be exporting a certain class of razors to Germany, although their cost of production here is *greater* that in Germany !

I dwell on this case merely in order to show how paradoxical is the subject of Foreign Trade, and what a mistake it is to be led away by cheap arguments which are really of a very superficial and delusive character.

You will find a careful exposition of the above subject in J. S. Mill's *Principles of Political Economy*, Book III, ch. xvii, § 2, from which I may as well give some extracts. Quoting his father, Mr. James Mill, he says : " If the cloth produced with 100 days' labor in Poland was produced with 150 days' labor in England, while the corn produced in Poland with 100 days' labor could not be produced in England with less than 200 days' labor ;—then an adequate motive to exchange would immediately arise. With a quantity of cloth which England produced with 150 days' labor, she would be able to purchase as much corn in Poland as was there produced with 100 days' labor ; but the quantity which was there produced with

100 days' labor would be as great as the quantity produced in England with 200 days' labor."

Then he continues: " By importing corn, therefore, from Poland, and paying for it with cloth, England would obtain for 150 days' labor what would otherwise cost 200, being a saving of 50 days' labor on each repetition of the transaction, and not merely a saving to England, but a saving absolutely ; for it is not obtained at the expense of Poland, who, with corn that costs her 100 days' labor, has purchased cloth which, if produced at home, would have cost her the same. Poland, therefore, on this supposition, loses nothing ; but also she derives no advantage from the trade, the imported cloth costing her as much as if it were made at home. To enable Poland to gain anything by the interchange, something must be abated from the gain of England—the corn produced in Poland by 100 days' labor must be able to purchase from England more cloth than Poland could produce by that amount of labor ; more, therefore, than England could produce by 150 days' labor, England thus obtaining the corn which would have cost her 200 days' at a cost exceeding 150, though short of 200. England, therefore, no longer gains the whole of the labor which is saved to the two jointly by trading with one another."

I would say in conclusion that though I am in favour of the institution of Wages Boards, etc., I think all this legislation which is being proposed with regard to Sweating, etc., is a very detestable thing. The evils of legislation generally are very obvious : Interference, Inspection, Expense, Officialism ; and it is only because they are a cure for worse evils that we must endure them for a time. We have got our social system and social habits into such an inhuman state that I suppose we shall have to go through a painful period of social drill and discipline and interference with individual liberty before better and more human ways of treating each other will become natural to us.

When Lafcadio Hearn—that greatest of writers on the subject of Japan—first visited that country he was struck, as most travelers are, by the extraordinary atmosphere of consideration, kindness, and civility to each other which existed there, by the general devotion to the common good, by the absence of poverty, and so forth. In his latest book (*Japan : An Interpretation*) he traces this state of affairs, which now appears spontaneous and natural, to the fact that in past centuries the people went through a period of considerable discipline in these directions, which, in fact, ingrained these habits into their lives.

Let us hope that the period through which *we* are now passing is one in which the Western nations are waking up to the enforcement of a more human morality in matters of Wealth and Industry than has existed heretofore ; and that it will result in a period in which such laws will *not* be necessary—because it will have become natural and instinctive for the employer to do his best for the employed, and because folk will have ceased to care for Wealth which has been obtained through the misery and degradation of others ; also perhaps because in *Co-operation* the distinction between employers and employed will have ceased to exist.